THE INDIAN TRIAL

Satank
National Archives

Satanta (White Bear)
Archives & Manuscripts
Division of the Oklahoma
Historical Society

THE INDIAN TRIAL

The Complete Story of the
Warren Wagon Train Massacre
and the
Fall of the Kiowa Nation

by
CHARLES M. ROBINSON, III

University of Oklahoma Press
Norman

Library of Congress Cataloging-in-Publication Data

Robinson, Charles M., 1949–
    The Indian Trial: the complete story of the Warren Wagon Train massacre and the fall c
the Kiowa Nation / by Charles Robinson

    p. 208 cm.

    Includes bibliographical references and index.

    LIBRARY OF CONGRESS CATALOG CARD NUMBER 96-32479

    ISBN 978-0-8061-5219-6 (paper)

    1. Warren Wagon Train Massacre, Tex., 1871. 2. Massacres—Texas-Young Country—
History—19th century/ 3. Kiowa Indians—Wars, conditions. 4. Kiowa Indians—Government
relations. 5. Kiowa Indians—Social conditions. 6. Satank, Kiowa Chief, 1810-1871. 7. Satanta,
Kiowa Chief, d. 1878. 8. Texas—History—19th century. I. Title.

E83.866R63 1997
976.4'545061 - dc 20   96-32479
                                                                                   CIP

The paper in this book meets the guidelines for permanence and durability of the Committee on
Production Guidelines for Book Longevity of the Council on Library Resources, Inc. ∞

In Memory of Doris and Whit

Contents

Illustrations

9

Author's Note

When I first sat down to write this history of the Jacksboro Indian Trial, I thought it would be a relatively straightforward account that would take a few weeks. After all, I already knew the story. Or at least, I thought I did.

As I delved into the story, however, I found it was much more than simply a massacre, followed by trial, imprisonment and parole of the guilty parties. Instead, it is a complex event in our history. It is the story of a proud, stubborn culture in its death throes against a determined, modern society which had no place for any system but its own. It is the story of Byzantine intrigues, and of high ideals which degenerated into criminal self-righteousness.

In assembling the vast amount of material scattered in archives all over the country, I was confronted with how much of the story to tell. I could have given a far more detailed account of the arrest of the three Kiowa chiefs. But that belongs with the story of Fort Sill, which Wilbur S. Nye has covered so thoroughly. I could have quoted Satanta's speech in the Everett House in St. Louis, but that is more properly part of his biography. Instead, I chose to give a general overview of the Warren Wagon Train Massacre, the trial of the chiefs, and its impact on national affairs, particularly those affecting the Southern Plains Indians.

There are no heroes or villains to this story. However, two men tower above all the rest. Ironically, these men have often been portrayed in the past as caught up in events they neither understood nor controlled. I have found the opposite to be true. One is Lawrie Tatum, the tough, brilliant Quaker who ran the Kiowa-Comanche Agency. Recent works are finally beginning to recognize his real position in the affair, and I hope I have been able to add a little. The second is Edmund J. Davis, the Radical Republican governor of Texas during Reconstruction. No true Southerner approves of Davis' administration, and I am a true Southerner. He was Radical to his fingertips, and followed the Reconstruction policy of running the state to satisfy its federal conquerors. But in this instance at least, Davis was no federal lackey. The time-worn portrayal of him handing over the Kiowa chiefs on demand is not only unfair, it is wrong. Davis was the main stumbling block in the federal-Quaker plan to liberate the Kiowas. Not only did he refuse to knuckle under, he went on the offensive. Before he was finished, the Department of the Interior had been forced to acknowledge Texas' sovereignty, and practically had to beg the state for the prisoners. This was all the more remarkable when one considers that Texas was essentially an occupied territory, and that ultimately Davis would have to give in. Although history does not owe him an apology, it certainly owes him a reexamination.

The Warren Wagon Train Massacre was—and is—an emotional issue. My work will settle nothing. Hopefully, though, it will provide some understanding of the people involved.

Many, many people and organizations were involved with this work. At the risk of omitting some, I wish to acknowledge those whose contribution to my study of the Kiowas has been extensive and consistent.

Special thanks to Betty J. Washburn (At-me-ponya San-kadota) of Apache, Oklahoma, Satanta's great-great-granddaughter, for her insights on Kiowa history and culture, as well as the history of her own family.

Thanks also to Dr. Robert Pierce, director of the Texas Prison Museum in Huntsville, for the time he spent with me going over the lore and facts of the Indian Trial.

I also wish to acknowledge the continual assistance of Robert Clark, The Arthur H. Clark Co., my mother, Rosalyn C. Robinson; and my wife, Perla.

The following organizations and individuals were very helpful with this project:

Texas—Austin: Texas State Library and Archive; Texas State Historical Association; Thomas A. Munnerlyn, State House Press; Center for American History, University of Texas. Canyon: Panhandle Plains Historical Society. Albany: Old Jail Art Center and Archive. Brownsville: Arnulfo Oliveira Library, University of Texas at Brownsville. Edinburg: Inter-library Loan Service, University Library, University of Texas-Pan American. Jacksboro: Jack County District Clerk's Office; Judy Rayburn, Fort Richardson State Historical Park. San Benito: San Benito Public Library. Lubbock: Southwestern Collection, Texas Tech University. Graham: Barbara A. Ledbetter, Fort Belknap.

Oklahoma—Oklahoma City: Oklahoma State Historical Society. Norman: University of Oklahoma Press. Tulsa: Thomas Gilcrease Institute. Stillwater: John Joerschke, Western Publications.

Kansas—Topeka: Kansas State Historical Society.

Washington, D.C.—National Archives; Library of Congress.

San Benito, Texas
March 1996

A Note on Kiowa Names

Romanized Kiowa is like Romanized Chinese in that the traditional spellings only approximate the actual sounds. Thus "Satanta" would be more accurately rendered "Set-t'aiñte," and "Satank" would be "Set-"añgya." I have used the traditional spellings throughout.

There is no rhyme or reason to the translations of the names. Satanta means "White Bear" and Satank is "Sitting Bear." But no one in Texas or Oklahoma calls them that, so their Kiowa names are used. The same applies to the medicine man Maman-ti. On the other hand A'do-eete has always been called "Big Tree", and for that reason I have used his English name. Likewise, Kicking Bird (whose Kiowa name, T'ené-agópte, actually means "Eagle Who Strikes With Talons"), White Horse, Lone Wolf, etc.

Oddly enough, "Satanta" is sometimes mispronounced "Santana." This even extends to official designations such as Santana's Face, a rock formation in Palo Duro Canyon State Park, which resembles the profile of the Kiowa chief. In fact, "Santana" is nothing more than a contraction of the Spanish "Santa Ana" (Saint Anne) and has no connection with the Kiowa word at all.

Abbreviations

AG	Adjutant General
AAG	Acting Adjutant General
AGO	Office of the Adjutant General
MilDivMo	Military Division of the Missouri
RG	Record Group
USA	United States Army

The Indian Trial

Part 1: The Kiowas and the Texans

CHAPTER 1

"When We Settle Down We Grow Pale and Die"

The Kiowas and the Texans had much in common. Both were newcomers who arrived in Texas about the same time. The Kiowas came from the northwest, around the area north of the Yellowstone. The first wave of white Texans came from the south, below the Rio Grande. Both groups pushed aside the native tribes as they sought to establish themselves in the harsh new country which each claimed for his own. Both clashed with other new arrivals of their own kind. Kiowas fought Comanches until they finally formed an uneasy alliance. The whites from the south came under the domination of whites from the east.

The story of white settlement in Texas is too well-known to repeat here. It remains to examine the Kiowa settlement, the events which led to the Warren Wagon Train Massacre of May 18, 1871, and the final subjugation of the Kiowa nation.

The traditional homeland of the Kiowas appears to have been the extreme headwaters of the Missouri River in what is now western Montana. They probably began their migrations in the seventeenth century, in a large-scale movement that occurred over several generations. An apparent vanguard of Kiowa raiders was mentioned by the Spaniards in the Southwest as early as 1732, while the major part of the tribe was still in the Platte River area on the northern plains. At some point, they came into contact with the Crows, with whom they allied

19

themselves about 1700. From the Crows, they acquired horses which gave them the mobility to shift from hunter-gatherers to warriors. They also adopted the plains Indian Sun Dance and began organizing warrior societies such as the Koiet-senko, who were the ten bravest men of the tribe.[1]

By about 1775 or 1780, they were living in the Black Hills of South Dakota, where they formed a permanent alliance with a small Athapaskan tribe which would henceforth be called the Kiowa-Apache, although they have no association with the Apache of the Southwest.[2] The Black Hills, however, were also claimed by the powerful and far more numerous Sioux, who forced out the Kiowas and Kiowa-Apache and pushed them south across the Arkansas River. Here they came into conflict with another tribe of refugees from the Sioux, a Shoshonean group called the Comanche. Both were mounted and aggressive, and once they were beyond the Sioux threat Kiowa and Comanche turned on each other in a fight for supremacy over the new territory. A series of exhausting wars ensued in which neither side gained the advantage until finally, about 1790, the two groups formed a loose confedera-tion that was to last until the end of the Indian Wars.[3]

Although the Kiowa-Comanche alliance was permanent, it had shortcomings. The Kiowas were a mystical, priestly peo-ple with a complex system of gods and spirits. Their lives were dominated by the supernatural. Oracles, omens, dreams and signs determined every aspect of a person's life, including whether or not he should join a war party. Coupled with that was a natural penchant for politics that frequently split them into various feuding factions. Singly or together, these two characteristics often tried the patience of the secular and prag-matic Comanches.[4]

---

[1]Mooney, *Calendar History,* 152-56.   [2]Ibid., 156-57; Mooney, "Kiowa," 1:699.
[3]Mayhall, *Kiowas,* 8-15; Newcomb, *Indians,* 194; Mooney, "Kiowa," 1:699, and *Calendar History,* 163-64.   [4]Newcomb, *Indians,* 210-11.

Lawrie Tatum, detail from view of
the General Superintendency, 1872.
*Archives & Manuscripts Division
of the Oklahoma Historical Society.*

Lawrie Tatum, agent to the Kiowas from 1869 to 1873,
wrote of a sinister aspect of the Kiowa religion, a mandate
given them by a mythological supreme being who was represented by the constellation of the Pleiades. A creator and
teacher who showed the Kiowas how to make bows, arrows
and household utensils, and called forth the buffalo for their
specific benefit, this being also foretold the coming of the
white men, whom they were to regard as enemies. This
injunction, Tatum believed, was partly responsible for the
Kiowas' reputation as raiders.[5] But ethnologist James Mooney,
who probably understood the tribe better than any other nineteenth century white, disputes a single "Great Spirit" concept,
stating instead that the Pleiades were "Star Girls," patronesses
of a women's ritual.[6]

Whether or not a "Great Spirit" was involved, Kiowa society was a marauding society, which was to soak the Texas

[5]Tatum, *Red Brothers*, 157.
[6]Mooney, *Calendar History*, 237, 239.

21

plains in blood. In an article about Kiowas for the *Handbook of American Indians North of Mexico*, Mooney wrote, "Among all the prairie tribes they were noted as the most predatory and bloodthirsty, and have probably killed more white men in proportion to their numbers than any of the others."[7]

A backward people using a culture largely borrowed and adapted, the Kiowas created little of their own except a complex diplomacy that was Byzantine in its duplicity. James Will Myers, a lieutenant of the 10th Cavalry posted to Fort Sill in the early 1870s, noted that the Kiowa's "language is as rough as his manner, and his heart is as cruel as it is fearless. His women are his slaves whom he may starve or beat to death unrestrained by any law of God or man known to him."[8]

The Kiowa language is a member of the Tanoan group and is related to several languages used in the New Mexico pueblos. Mooney describes it as "full of nasal and choked sounds...not well adapted to rhythmic composition."[9] In spite of that, the Kiowas were gifted orators, and in conferences between Indians and government officials they invariably were called on to speak for the various assembled tribes. In such cases, they used Comanche, the generally acknowledged court language of the Southern Plains.

Orators to the Indians, they were merciless raiders against the Texans, sweeping down first against the Spaniards and the Mexicans, and then against the English-speaking Easterners. Themselves aliens to the land, they ranged far across Texas beyond their own pale, and deep into Mexico; they were not defending territory, they were marauding. For above all else, the Kiowas had become a warrior people, and gained merit according to their proficiency with a scalping knife. And as the Texans pushed westward, establishing themselves first in

---

[7]Mooney, "Kiowa," 1:699.
[8]Myers, Papers.
[9]Mooney, "Kiowa," 1:700.

the Kiowa raiding areas and later moving into the Kiowas' own hunting grounds, lonely, isolated ranches presented the Indians with an ideal situation. Never numbering more than a few hundred warriors at the height of their power, they attacked only where they had overwhelming superiority. This was not cowardice but survival. When a Kiowa warrior fell, it would take a generation to replace him. They simply could not afford serious losses.

The annexation of Texas to the United States presented them with a peculiar and confusing situation. To begin with, their quarrel was with the Texans, whom they regarded as a distinct people separate from the Americans. Secondly, they had no desire for confrontation with the federal government, realizing that every bluecoated soldier they killed would be immediately replaced by others. They never understood why the American soldiers took offense at their depredations. After all, they had remained neutral in the government's conflicts with the Osages and the Utes, since it did not concern them. Why then did the United States interfere with their raids into Texas?[10] Thus the Kiowas were reasonably quiet north of the Red River, and were murderers, rapists and thieves south of it. The lonely settler of the Texas plains learned to dread the coming of spring. With tall grass for their ponies, and warm, moonlit nights, the Kiowas ranged far and wide.

In 1853, the federal government executed one of a series of treaties with the Kiowas and their allies at Fort Atkinson, Kansas. The primary motive was to protect the Santa Fe Trail. To this end it was willing to pay an annuity of $18,000 a year for ten years, with an option to extend it for another five years.

---

[10]Myers, Papers. Although Myers considered the Indians backward and primitive, he respected them as human beings and was sympathetic to many of their grievances. In Folder 10 of his papers, he wrote a hypothetical interview with the average Indian in an effort to present both sides of the conflict. Myers ultimately was dismissed from the army and established a law practice in Fort Griffin, Texas, where he was fatally wounded by a stray bullet during a saloon brawl in January 1877.

In turn, the tribes recognized the shifts in national boundaries caused by the Mexican War, and agreed to the building of roads and military posts in their territory. In deference to the Mexicans, the government attempted to gain a guarantee from the Kiowas that they would cease raiding in Mexico and would surrender Mexican prisoners. Here the Indians balked. Most Mexicans had been captured as children, had been absorbed into the tribe, and were not particularly willing to leave. Nor were the Kiowas willing to give them up. When they finally signed, they did so without the slightest intention of honoring the agreement on prisoners.

The Kiowa signer was Satank, leader of the Koiet-senko, the bravest of the brave. A private of the dragoons found him particularly impressive, describing him as "a man about five feet ten, sparely made, muscular, cat-like in his movements—more Spanish than Indian in his appearance—spare features, thin lips, keen restless eyes, thin mustache and scattering chin whiskers that seemed to have stopped growing when one to three inches long...."[11] Although one of their leading chiefs, Satank was feared and disliked by the Kiowas, who spoke of his vindictiveness, and believed he used occult powers against those who displeased him.[12] Still, he was respected as a Koiet-senko and, in council, his words carried weight.

A rising personality at this time was Satanta. Younger than Satank, he was large and muscular. Whereas the Koeit-senko was quiet and deliberate, Satanta was a natural showman with a gift for public relations. Yet there was no bluff behind his posturing arrogance; his talents as a warrior and a leader were very real. One of his trademarks was a bugle he had apparently taken during a skirmish with soldiers. He learned a few calls and used it to signal warriors during fights. Although other

---

[11]Lowe, *Five Years a Dragoon*, 131. Lowe used the name "Satanta," but the physical description is of Satank. Contemporary writers often confused the two.

[12]Mooney, *Calendar History*, 329.

Indians also carried them, Satanta was the most famous, and on the southern plains, frontiersmen who heard the sound of a bugle during an Indian attack came to assume he was present.

Satanta used his bugle often enough because throughout the 1850s, Kiowas and whites skirmished and snapped at each other, the major point of contention being the raids into Texas and Mexico. The federal government authorized punitive expeditions, and there were occasional pitched battles between Indian and white. But the open warfare came about due to a completely unrelated event: the outbreak of the Civil War. When Texas joined the Southern cause, federal property was surrendered to local authorities and United States troops were withdrawn. State militia and Confederate troops soon were called to the battlefields of Virginia and Maryland, leaving the frontier unprotected. Secession reenforced the Kiowa belief that Americans and Texas were two distinct peoples. Encouraged now by the federal government "to do all the damage they could to Texas, because Texas was at war with the United States," the plains tribes swept down on the settlements.[13]

Satanta led raids as far into Texas as Menard, then retreated back up into Kansas. In 1864, the Kiowas and Comanches laid waste to Young County in one of the worst raids in Texas history, carrying off both white and black prisoners. Most of the captives were later ransomed through the efforts of Britt Johnson, a heroic black slave. But one child, Millie Durkin or Durgan, simply disappeared.[14] The few federal troops along

---

[13]Ibid., 177, 180.

[14]The Young County raid and Britt Johnson were the bases of Matt Braun's 1972 novel, *Black Fox*, which was adapted as a television mini-series on CBS in 1995. In 1930, an elderly Kiowa woman appeared in Young County, convinced that she was Millie Durkin. She was obviously white, but had been with the Indians so long she remembered no other existence. At the time, she was accepted as Millie, but this has since been discredited. No one knows who she was, other than one of the many nameless Texas children who vanished into Indian captivity during the plains wars. See Ledbetter, *Fort Belknap*, 1-13.

the northern frontier found themselves in a virtual state of siege, powerless to prevent the depredations. By the time United States authority was reestablished in Texas in 1865, the frontier line of defense had been pushed a hundred miles east of its 1860 limit.

Faced with pressure from the East to appease the Indians, the federal government negotiated the Treaty of the Little Arkansas with the Kiowas, Comanches and Kiowa-Apaches in 1865. The Kiowa signatories were their paramount chief, Dohasen, himself a moderate, Lone Wolf, Satank and Kicking Bird, the latter also a moderate but without the power of Dohasen. Under the terms of the treaty, the tribes agreed to accept a reservation including the Texas Panhandle and all of the Indian Territory west of the 98th meridian, along with regular annuities. To make sure they stayed there, the government ringed the area with military posts, including Fort Richardson, just outside the little town of Jacksboro, Texas.

The treaty had several flaws. To begin with, the greatest of the plains tribes were bitter over the recent massacre of Black Kettle's Cheyennes at Sand Creek in Colorado, and boycotted the conference. Secondly, the federal government did not have the legal authority to cede any land in Texas. The forts, however widely separated, represented confinement to the Indians. But most damaging of all was the corrupt annuity system that allowed the many unscrupulous agents and their political patrons to reap fortunes at Indian expense.[15]

The Seminole Chief Billy Bowlegs described annuity day to a correspondent of the Louisville *Journal,* who wrote:

> The Indian Agent makes his appearance at a certain point to distribute the annuities. The Indians of the tribe, having been previously notified, are present. A young warrior, in the first flush of manhood, ambitious, inexperienced, comes up to receive say $100,

---

[15]Hamilton, "Military History," 68-69; Jones, *Treaty of Medicine Lodge,* 10.

26

which is due him as the son of a chief. The first thing that attracts him is a beautiful blanket, a red Mah-kee-nah [Mackinaw] perhaps, which the artful agent has placed in a prominent position for the very purpose. He must have that blanket. Very well; the agent is willing that he should; it is just the same as money. A roll is prepared in blank, but the ignorant Indian does not know it. He makes his mark. Then the blank is filled by the agent with as many blankets as he deems prudent. Our Seminole has known of instances where the blank has been filled with forty blankets, while only one was actually received by the Indian receipting.

There are butcher knives, a very nice article. An Indian who wishes one is charged $40 for it. If he gets drunk and wishes to return it to get something else, he is the same day permitted to return it, and is credited with $1.25.

Presently the agent, finding that his receipts will cover the whole annuity to the tribe, suddenly closes his books, and announces to the crestfallen Indians that there is no more to come. But he has still on hand a few blankets and other trifles for which he will dicker. If an Indian would like an old French musket, for which the agent has paid $3, he can have it for $45 in cash, or furs at the lowest price. So the shameless trade goes on. At night the agent has full receipts for his goods or cash, and has seven-eighths of the whole safe in his pocket or under guard. Perhaps he will have large portions of it exposed for sale on the frontier shortly afterward. Perhaps he will have it safely buried at his encampment.

Now, if he can get all the Indians drunk he can probably steal back the greater portion of the one-eighth distributed to them. Next day he will swear they traded with him for whisky. So he rolls out a dozen kegs of whisky, knocks out the heads, and winds up the day with the biggest spree he can get up.

This is the model Indian agent, painted from life.[16]

By 1867, the plains tribes were uneasy again. Dohasen had died in the spring of the previous year. Of all the moderate chiefs, only he had the prestige to enforce his will over the Kiowas as a whole, and his death left a void. His successor to the paramount chieftaincy, Lone Wolf, was a member of the

---

[16]Louisville *Journal* quoted in New York *Times*, October 3, 1867.

war faction. Direct white pressure, particularly the construction of the transcontinental railroad, was also a factor in the general restlessness, as were jurisdictional disputes between the War Department, charged with keeping peace on the frontier, and the Department of the Interior, responsible for the Indians. But much was due to feuding among the Indians themselves. White expansion elsewhere funneled more and more tribes into the plains. There was less freedom of movement for the normally nomadic people, and traditional enemies were thrown together. Texas, which had entered the Union as a sovereign republic with control over its own territory, refused to surrender the vast Panhandle area that the federal government had illegally promised as a reservation. Satanta and the other war chiefs returned to raiding.

Public pressure mounted for a new treaty. On July 30, 1867, President Andrew Johnson signed a bill calling for a new peace commission to meet with the plains tribes. The commission would consist of Senator John B. Henderson of Missouri, chairman of the Committee on Indian Affairs and author of the bill; N.G. Taylor, commissioner of Indian Affairs; Samuel F. Tappan, who had headed a military investigation of the Sand Creek Massacre; John B. Sandborn, who had represented the Department of the Interior at the Little Arkansas Treaty, and military representatives. One major factor set this treaty commission apart from all those that had gone before. It was not only to negotiate peace on the frontier and passage for the railroad, but also "establish a system for civilizing the tribes." In other words, the Indians were no longer to be pushed aside. There would now be an effort to convert them over to white values and fit them into society.[17]

The council was to convene by Medicine Lodge Creek in Kansas, which many of the Southern Plains tribes used as a winter encampment. In terms of the insular American

---

[17]Hamilton, "Military History," 69-70; Jones, *Medicine Lodge*, 11-17.

society of the times, it was perhaps as important as today's summits of superpowers. The government was, in fact, negotiating with tribes whose combined strength seriously threatened internal security. Consequently, when the commissioners arrived at Fort Larned, some sixty miles north of Medicine Lodge, they were accompanied by a substantial press corps. Among them was Henry Morton Stanley, then a correspondent for the St. Louis *Missouri Democrat*, later to gain fame in Africa, who published perhaps the most detailed account of the gathering.

The delegation was met at the fort by a group of leading chiefs, among whom was Satanta. He had been introduced to Stanley earlier that year and greeted him with a bear hug. Stanley, in turn, presented him to the other members of the press corps.

"By his defiant and independent bearing he attracted all eyes," Stanley wrote. "He would certainly be a formidable enemy to encounter alone on the prairie. It is said that he has 'killed more white men than any other Indian on the plains.'" But as drinks went around, even Satanta became cheerful and laughed along with the whites.[18]

The commissioners left the post on October 12. Stanley counted 165 wagons and ambulances. Satanta rode in the lead wagon with Major General William Harney, the War Department representative. The congeniality soon was broken by white thoughtlessness. Orders had been given that no firearms were to be discharged in the Indians' country. But the sight of a herd of buffalo was too much for some hangers-on in the party. They shot down several animals, cut out the tongues and left the carcasses to rot. That was more than Satanta was willing to tolerate. The destruction of the buffalo was a sore point which the Indians raised at every peace council, and he was not going to let this incident pass.

---

[18]Stanley, *Travels and Adventures*, 223-24.

"Has the white man become a child, that he should reck-lessly kill and not eat?" he asked with scorn. "When the red men slay game, they do so that they may live and not starve."

Harney got the point. The malefactors were placed under arrest, as was Major Joel Elliott, the officer in charge of the military escort, who had failed to prevent the incident.[19]

The council opened at 10 a.m. Saturday, October 19. Some 400 chiefs gathered, representing Kiowas, Comanches, Ara-pahos, Southern Cheyennes, Osages, and various other plains tribes. The principal chiefs sat in a half-circle facing the com-missioners, with the Kiowas on the left. Satanta sat in front on an army camp stool, and wearing a military jacket he had received from Harney when they had met at Fort Larned the previous spring. He was about fifty years old and in his prime. Immediately behind him were the Koiet-senko Satank, now about seventy and growing gray, but as tough as ever. He was wearing a Peace Medal with a portrait of President James Buchanan. Next to him was Kicking Bird, whose influence was rising. Although Kicking Bird never attained the author-ity of old Dohasen, he was a power to be reckoned with in Kiowa politics.[20]

Of all the chiefs, Satanta made the greatest impression on the New York *Times* representative, who wrote:

> It must be remembered than in cunning or native diplomacy SATANTA has no equal. In worth and influence RED CLOUD is his rival; but in boldness, daring and merciless cruelty SATANTA is far superior, and yet there are some good points in this dusky chief-tain which command admiration. If a white man does him an injury he never forgives him; but if on the other hand the white man has done him a service, death alone can prevent him from paying the debt.

---

[19]Ibid., 225-29; Jones, *Medicine Lodge*, 66-68; New York *Times*, October 19, 1867, Octo-ber 26, 1867.

[20]Jones, *Medicine Lodge*, 11; New York *Times*, October 30, 1867.

CHAPTER 1: "...WE GROW PALE AND DIE"

The government's spokesman, Senator Henderson, waived the usual formalities and got down to business. He told the chiefs that the United States expected peace and would address tribal grievances, and that the commissioners would select lands for their farms, and would build schools and churches for them.

Satanta replied on behalf of the Kiowas and Comanches. Unlike Henderson, he spent several minutes on diplomatic niceties. Then he made his point.

> All the land south of the Arkansas belongs to the Kiowas and Comanches, and I don't want to give away any of it. I love the land and the buffalo, and will not part with it. I want you to understand well what I say. Write it on paper. Let the Great Father see it, and let me hear what he has to say. I want you to understand, also, that the Kiowas and Comanches don't want to fight, and have not been fighting since we made the treaty [of the Little Arkansas]. I hear a good deal of good talk from the gentlemen whom the Great Father sends us, but they never do what they say. I don't want any of the Medicine lodges [schools] within the country. I want the children raised as I was. When I make peace, it is a long and lasting one; there is no end to it.

As he spoke, Satanta grew more forceful. His voice rising to a frenzy, he almost shouted:

> I have heard that you intend to settle us on a reservation near the mountains. I don't want to settle. I love to roam over the prairies. I feel free and happy; but when we settle down we grow pale and die...I have told you the truth. I have no little lies hid about me; but I don't know how it is with the Commissioners. Are they as clear as I am? A long time ago this land belonged to our fathers; but when I go up to the river I see camps of soldiers on its banks. These soldiers cut down my timber, they kill my buffalo; and when I see that my heart feels like bursting; I feel sorry.

Much of the land Satanta contested was in Kansas, and Governor Samuel J. Crawford and Senator Edmund Ross, both of whom were present, would hear none of it. Their

31

views were plain. They would oppose any appeasement that involved Kansas. Satanta was equally stubborn and was backed by the Comanche Chief Ten Bears. Each side was playing for time, hoping that the commission's tight schedule would force a decision in its favor.

As discussions progressed, the Indians had an internal dispute that almost wrecked the conference. In their usual fashion, the Kiowas had to debate each issue among themselves before announcing a decision. Arguments had to be heard, compromises reached, deals made. Ten Bears grew impatient, and remarked to one of the white commissioners, "What I say is law for the Comanches, but it takes half-a-dozen to speak for the Kiowas."

Satanta exploded. He and Ten Bears got into a heated argument. Henderson tried to restore order, but to no avail. Satanta stormed out of the conference in a fury.

In the end, the Indians gave in. Ten Bears said the Comanches would consider a reservation if the Texans were kept out of it. Satanta added that the size of the tribes would require a separate reservation for each, indicating that otherwise, they might get on each other's nerves. He also stressed that annuities would have to be distributed honestly and on schedule. That point hit a sore spot, and one for which the government had no answer. In the case of the Kiowas, Agent Jesse Leavenworth had been instructed by his superiors to withhold annuities until all white captives had been released without ransom. If the government negotiators at Medicine Lodge knew this, they elected not to admit it, leaving the impression that annuities delivered to the Kiowas under the Little Arkansas Treaty had fallen far short of the amounts promised. Satanta believed Leavenworth personally responsible for withholding the annuities, and said so. The two men had long disliked each other, and this was not the first time

32

Satanta had made public accusations against the agent. Commissioner Taylor replied that the goods for the current year were in the government camp and would be distributed at the end of that day's deliberations. The Kiowas received their full share. In spite of the distasteful treaty terms, Satanta had scored a major diplomatic victory.[21]

The Kiowas and the Comanches signed the treaty on October 21. A last minute provision maintained Indian hunting rights in the Texas Panhandle, something that, once again, the federal government had no right to grant. In turn, the Indians agreed to share a large reservation by the Wichita Mountains in the southwest Indian Territory. Satanta, Satank and Kicking Bird were among the nine Kiowa signatories.

Now it was Satank's turn. Throughout the proceedings, the old Koiet-senko had sat quietly, while Satanta did the talking. In fact, Satanta had said so much that the press corps dubbed him the "Orator of the Plains", with more sarcasm than its northern and eastern readers realized. But while Satanta may have left the most lasting impression on the whites, the Kiowas were waiting to hear Satank who, despite their ill feelings toward him, had the greatest prestige of all. Once the annuities had been distributed, he led a hundred warriors to the commissioners' tent.

Weighing his words carefully as he spoke, he began:

> It has made me glad to meet you who are the Commissioners of the Great Father. You no doubt are tired of the much talk of our people Many of them have put ourselves forward and filled you with their sayings. I have kept back and said nothing, not that I did not consider myself still the principal [war] Chief of the Kiowa Nation, but others younger than I desired to talk and I left it to them. Before leaving, however, as I now intend to go, I come to say that the

---

[21]Stanley, *Travels and Adventures*, 233; Thomas Murphy, Superintendent of Indian Affairs, to J.H. Leavenworth, October 9, 1866, RG 393, Special File, MilDivMo, Hancock's War; Jones, *Medicine Lodge*, 124-25; New York *Times*, October 30, 1867.

Kiowas and Comanches have made with you a peace, and they intend to keep it. If it brings prosperity to us we of course will like it the better. If it brings prosperity or adversity we will not abandon it. It is our contract and it shall stand. Our people once carried war against Texas. We though the Great father would not be offended, for the Texans had gone out from among his people and become his enemies.[22] You now tell us that they have made peace and returned to the great family. The Kiowas and Comanches will now make no bloody trail in their land. They have pledged their word and that word shall last, unless the whites shall break their contract and invite the horrors of war. We do not break treaties. We make but few contracts and them we remember well. The whites make so many that they are liable to forget them. The white chief seems not able to govern his braves. The Great Father seems powerless in the face of his children. He sometimes becomes angry when he sees the wrongs of his people committed on the red man, and his voice becomes loud as the roaring winds. But like the wind, it soon dies away and leaves the sullen calm of unheeded oppression. We hope now that a better time has come. If all would talk and then do as you have done, the sun of peace would shine forever. We have warred against the white man, but never because it gave us pleasure. Before the day of our oppression came, no white man came to our villages and went away hungry. It gave us more joy to share with him than it gave him to partake of our hospitality. In the far distant past there was no suspicion among us. The world seemed large enough for both the red and the white man. Its broad plains seem now to contract, and the white man grows jealous of his red brother. He once came to trade; he now comes as a soldier. He once put his trust in our friendship, and wanted no shield but our fidelity, but now he builds forts and plants big guns on their walls. He once gave us arms and powder, and bade us to hunt the game; we then loved him for his confidence; he now suspects our plighted faith and drives us to be his enemies. He now covers his face with the cloud of jealousy and anger, and tells us to be gone, as the offended master speaks to his dog.

Pointing to the Peace Medal around his neck, he said:

Look at this medal I wear. By wearing this, I have been made

---

[22]By this, Satank referred to Texas secession.

poor. Before, I was rich in horses and lodges. Today I am the poorest of all. When you gave me this silver medal on my neck, you made me poor. We thank the Great Spirit that all these wrongs are now to cease, and the old day of peace and friendship [is] to come again. You came as friends, you talked as friends, you have patiently heard our many complaints. To you they may have seemed trifling--to us they are everything. You have not tried, as many do, to get from us our lands for nothing. You have not tried to make a new bargain merely to get the advantage. You have not asked to make our annuities smaller; but unasked, you have made them larger. You have not withdrawn a single gift, but voluntarily you have provided new guarantees for our education and comfort. When we saw these things, we then said, these are the men of the past. We at once gave you our hearts. You have now have them. You know what is best for us. Do for us what is best. Teach us the road to travel and we will not depart from it forever. For your sakes the green grass shall not be stained with the blood of whites. Your people shall again be our people, and peace shall be our mutual heritage. If wrong comes we shall look for you for the right. We know you will not forsake us, and [will] tell your people to be as you have been. I am old, and will soon join my fathers; but those who come after me will remember this day. It is now treasured up by the old, and will be carried by them to the grave, and then handed down to be kept as a sacred tradition by their children, and their children's children. And now the time has come when I must go. Good bye! You may not see me again, but remember Satank as the white man's friend.

Satank's speech is considered the greatest ever made by a Plains Indian, and ranks along with those of Chiefs Joseph and John Logan. Joseph's surrender address was years in the future when the Medicine Lodge Treaty was signed. But the whites who heard Satank were ready to compare him with Logan. And while there is evidence that the latter's speech was edited and romanticized for popular consumption, there is no misunderstanding about Satank. Eight reporters and seven commissioners all agreed on what he said. Even the most violent Indian-haters of the group were moved. As they absorbed his words, the old warrior moved down the line, shaking hands with each man. Then he mounted his pony and rode away. After this, the treaties and speeches with the other tribes became anti-climactic.[23]

---

[23]Stanley, St. Louis *Missouri Democrat*, November 2, 1867; Brown, Cincinnati *Commercial*, November 4, 1867; New York *Times*, November 4, 1867. The *Times* erroneously attributed this speech to Satanta instead of Satank and the error has persisted into modern works; the oration itself is generally known as "Chief Satanta's Speech." However, correspondent George Brown of the *Commercial*, and Henry Stanley, both eyewitnesses to the scene, state unequivocally that the speaker was Satank. Stanley's word carries particular weight because he knew Satanta and Satank from previous meetings.

CHAPTER 2

"These Savage Visits Made by the Quaker Pets"

The federal government was determined to wipe out corruption in the annuity system. The Kiowas were determined to maintain their traditional lifestyle. And the Texans were determined to defend their homes.

At the outset, the federal government seemed to face the most difficult task of the three. The "Indian Ring," the eastern political and financial interests that profited from agency corruption and Indian war, was firmly entrenched in Washington. In the Department of the Interior, vast fortunes were made from annuities on the one hand, and sale of arms and ammunition to the Indians on the other. The civilian arm of the War Department was equally guilty. Unrest on the plains, raids, and the murder of settlers required a continuing military presence. The merchants and suppliers of garrison towns had much to gain from this, and the profiteers made sure a share of it filtered back to their patrons in the capital.

The San Antonio *Express* summed up the question as being "how to protect the Indians in their own reservations, and to prevent the inroads of white adventurers, who are taking away their lands without compensation, and introducing among them the worst forms of disease and demoralization that afflicts human nature."[1]

---

[1] San Antonio *Express*, February 9, 1871.

One group of people felt it had the answer. This was the Society of Friends—the Quakers—farmers, businessmen, and teachers. Hard workers, idealists, and thoroughly honest. In 1868, as Congress considered a bill to transfer the Indians to the jurisdiction of the War Department, the Orthodox Friends appointed a committee to consider solutions to the Indian question. Their inspiration was William Penn, who had dealt honestly with the Pennsylvania tribes, and whose policies had maintained peace in the white settlements there. In December 1868, the Friends Committee petitioned Congress to allow it to assume jurisdiction of the agencies in the Indian Territory. The following spring, General U.S. Grant, who succeeded Johnson as president, agreed to accept Quaker nominations for Indian agents.[2]

Grant had an ulterior motive for working with the Quakers. On March 3, 1869, Congress approved the Army Reduction Act, reducing the size of the standing army and creating a surplus of demobilized officers. Initially, the president believed that assigning these officers to the Indian service as superintendents and agents would reduce political influence and stem corruption in the system. General W.T. Sherman, commanding general of the army, believed this was "undoubtedly a change for the better, but most distasteful to members of Congress, who looked to these appointments as part of their patronage."[3]

The Indian Ring retaliated by securing congressional approval of a bill that vacated the commission of any military officer who served in a civil capacity. Informed by some members of Congress that this was deliberately intended to block the appointments of qualified military personnel to agency posts, Grant struck back by dividing the agencies among the

---

[2]Tatum, *Red Brothers*, 22-23.
[3]Sherman, *Memoirs*, 926-27.

churches, knowing that the congressmen dared not object. Accordingly, army officers were relieved of agency posts, and the various superintendencies were divided among the Quakers, Methodists, Catholics, Episcopalians, Presbyterians and other denominations.[4] Thus the agencies ceased being political prizes, becoming instead new outposts for evangelism. The Orthodox Friends were given the Superintendency in Lawrence, Kansas, comprising ten reservations with responsibility for some 17,724 Indians in Kansas and the Indian Territory.[5]

After Grant offered to accept Quaker nominations for agencies under the Lawrence superintendency, the Friends met in Indianapolis and concluded:

> It is our united judgment that we should recommend none but such as are deeply imbued with the love of Christ, and who feel willing to accept the position from Christian and not from mere mercenary motives—men fearing God and hating covetousness.

The resolution also said the new agents

> should be men of sound judgment and ready tact in managing such business as will necessarily claim their attention. Possessing, first, a practical knowledge of agriculture and general farm management; second, a capacity of financiering.

In other words, they were to teach the Indians, and make sure they got every dime the government allocated.

Enoch Hoag of Muscatine, Iowa, was named superintendent. Elsewhere in Iowa, a Quaker farmer named Lawrie Tatum learned from a newspaper that, without his knowledge, he had been nominated agent to the Kiowas, Comanches, Wichitas and "affiliated bands," and that his nomination had been confirmed by the Senate. In Tatum's own words, his new charges

---

[4]Ibid., 927.
[5]Prucha, *The Great Father* 161-62.

Superintendant E. Hoag.
*Archives & Manuscripts
Division of the Oklahoma
Historical Society.*

were still addicted to raiding in Texas, stealing horses and mules, and
sometimes committing other depredations, and especially this was
the case with the Kiowas and Comanches. They were probably the
worst Indians east of the Rocky Mountains.

Yet his Christian duty was clear, and on May 20, 1869, he met
Colonel W.B. Hazen, head of the Southern Indian Military
District, at Junction City, Kansas, who escorted him on the
long trip south to the agency some three or four miles from
the newly established post of Fort Sill. On July 1, the agency
was formally turned over to him.

Tatum soon learned the extent of his new charges' "addic-
tion" to raiding. For the Medicine Lodge Treaty had accomplished nothing on that score; the leading chiefs were still
making regular forays across the Red River. One chief told
him that if the president did not want the young warriors

raiding into Texas, then the president should move Texas far enough away that the young warriors couldn't find it.[6]

The Indians were quieter than usual in 1869, although there were some raids into the Texas frontier counties, such as Jack, Parker and Palo Pinto. In his annual report to the committee, Tatum said he believed the chiefs were making an honest effort to control the young warriors. But he added they were no more able to do that than established law enforcement was able to prevent crime in a civilized society.

One of the problems was the government's reversal of the policy used by Agent Leavenworth; it now tried to buy peace by issuing larger amounts of annuity goods to hostile bands than to those who remained peaceful. As Tatum noted:

> They repeatedly told me that when they behaved well they got but a small amount of goods, and the only way to get a large amount was to go on the war path a while, kill a few white people, and then make a treaty, and they would get a large amount of presents and a liberal supply of goods for that fall.

He went on to point out that the annuity for 1869 was one-fourth of the amount for the previous year, the explanation being that the balance had been charged against the tribes as reparations for raids prior to the Medicine Lodge Treaty. Coupled with this was the failure of the Indians as farmers. Not being used to produce, they ate corn, vegetables and melons before they were ripe, and many were sick because of it.

Given the difficulties in the relatively peaceful year of 1869, Tatum expected trouble in 1870. Consequently, he recommended large amounts of goods when the tribes had behaved, and withholding them when they were hostile. In addition, he and Colonel Benjamin Grierson, commander of the 10th

---

[6]Tatum, *Red Brothers*, 23-30.

Cavalry and of Fort Sill, agree to close the market for stolen livestock by prohibiting traders or citizens from purchasing horses and mules from the Indians.

"This prohibition makes it more difficult for the well disposed Indians to procure the necessaries of life," Tatum observed, "but under the circumstances we think it best. While the Indians have an open market to sell horses, many of them will steal them to supply the market."

In the spring of 1870, the tribe grew "restless and uneasy." Those who had raised crops the year before abandoned their farm plots. "They told me...that the next spring they would go to work at planting and cultivating their land. I believe they were aware that there was going to be trouble this summer," Tatum reported.[7]

In late May, the Kiowas held their annual Sun Dance which was attended by the Comanches and other plains tribes. Although the dance itself was purely religious, it signalled the start of a summer of raiding. The depredations began in the immediate vicinity of Fort Sill. Two men were shot, one of them fatally, not two hundred yards from the agency itself. The same morning, another party killed and scalped a man six miles away. Horses were stolen from the agency and from the corrals at Fort Sill itself.

Tatum knew his situation was dangerous. In June, he called a meeting of the Quakers assigned to the agency, and suggested they decide for themselves whether they should return to the States. Everyone left except Tatum and his wife, and Josiah and Lizzie Butler, the school teachers.[8]

It wasn't long before the raids spilled over into Texas. On June 2, Indians killed the mail driver between Fort Richardson and Fort Griffin, and carried off the mules and mail sacks.

---

[7]Second Annual Report, Office of the Kiowa and Comanche Agency, Fort Sill, August 12, 1870, manuscript copy in Myers Papers.

[8]Tatum, *Red Brothers*, 34-35.

42

Colonel Benjamin
Grierson. *National
Archives.*

About the same time, a Professor Roessler, geologist from the
Interior Department, left Fort Richardson with an escort of
Sixth Cavalry and several citizens of Jacksboro and Weatherford, to investigate some reported copper deposits about a
hundred miles to the northwest. As the party neared its destination, it was attacked. A soldier and two civilians were
killed.[9]

On July 11, a scouting expedition of fifty-six men from Fort
Richardson under command of Captain Curwin McClellan
was attacked in a valley along the Little Wichita, by some 250
agency Kiowas. McClellan dismounted to get the advantage
of stability in gunfire over the Indian horsemen, then began a

---

[9]Austin *Weekly State Journal,* June 16, 1870; McConnell, *Five Years a Cavalryman,* 215-
16.

Kicking Bird.
*Kansas State
Historical Society*

slow retreat. The fight lasted about eight hours until the Kiowas broke off for the night. The next morning, it was evident the Indians had left the field, and McClellan took his battered command back to the fort. Two soldiers were killed and fourteen wounded. Eighteen dead horses and some of the pack animals were abandoned. Later, McClellan passed through Fort Sill, where he learned the Indian losses had been "considerable."

Incredibly this attack had been led by Kicking Bird, some of whose braves had been responsible for the mail driver as well. The peace chief had fallen under increasing criticism at home, and his ability as a warrior had been questioned. For a Kiowa, this was intolerable. If he was to maintain any prestige at all,

44

he had to lead a raid. Then and only then could he show that his pacifism was due to conviction and not cowardice.[10]

The Fort Sill tribes were now completely out of control. White Horse led a foray into Montague County, where his braves killed a settler named Gottlieb Koozer, and carried his wife and children into captivity.[11]

The Texas press howled loud and long, and laid the blame for the frontier troubles squarely on the federal government and the Quakers. The Austin *Weekly State Journal* fumed:

> The Indian Bureau reports that the gentle savages on the reserve, are making satisfactory strides in civilization, and that all that is needed to make them unfledged cherubims [sic] are a few more grants and appropriations of money.
>
> Apropos to this, we learn that a number of these benign creatures who had been absent on a harmless (?) hunting trip to the frontiers of Texas, had returned to the agency *wounded.* Doubtless medicines, surgeons, and nurses will be hurried to them from Washington by express....
>
> The people of Jack, Parker and Montague counties, who have lost stock and horses, and can point to the new made graves of settlers, killed and scalped by these proteges of civilization, have a very keen and painful sense of these savage visits made by the Quaker pets on the government reservation, who are supplied by the United States with arms, clothing, and rations, and who make war on the citizens of Texas, carrying back to their homes, on the reserve, scalps, prisoners and horses.[12]

Although they summed up the attitude in Washington reasonably well, editorials such as this were hardly fair to Tatum and Grierson at Fort Sill. They were doing their best to defuse an impossible situation within constraints imposed by the government, and restrictions of their own consciences. Grierson, at least, could back his position with troops. Tatum, on

---

[10]McConnell, *Five Years A Cavalryman*, 216-17; Robinson, "Kicking Bird," 16.

[11]Nye, *Carbine and Lance*, 112.

[12]Austin *Weekly State Journal*, April 28, 1870.

the other hand, was prohibited by his religious beliefs from violence, either offensive or defensive. His only weapons were iron nerve and force of character.

On July 4, two Kiowas came to the agency to see if the Comanches might come in and draw rations. Tatum remembered the thefts at the agency and from the corrals at Fort Sill, and told them rations would be issued only if the stolen animals were returned. Six days later, he was told several chiefs had joined the hostile Quahadi Comanches, but the others wanted to come in. He repeated his demand for the livestock. The Indians replied that Kicking Bird was assembling the animals and would return them. Tatum said rations would be issued at that time, but would not include ammunition. He also decided to withhold half the allotment of coffee and sugar, two things the Indians most prized, as additional incentive for good behavior.

As he dealt with the tribes on rations, he was also making a serious effort to locate white prisoners. He managed to secure the release of the Koozer family, and was making inquiries on behalf of Patrick Field, a farmer in San Saba County, Texas, whose wife had been carried off in an 1864 raid. Tatum had no word on her, but hoped to get some information from Apaches due in soon. In an effort to reassure Field, he wrote:

> In obtaining Mrs. Koozer and her children, I had but few words with the Indians on the subject. I told them that they must bring them and deliver them to me before they got any more rations, and I would make them such presents as I saw proper. After they were delivered, I gave them one hundred dollars for each capture, thinking they would be less likely to kill their captives if they got some present for them. This is all they received for them. Since then, I have obtained Kilgore [Martin Kilgore, a captive Texas youth] in the same way.

Tatum did not bother to tell Field that as he demanded the

46

prisoners, one Indian kept loading and unloading his rifle, another was snapping arrows in his bow, and a third whetted his knife. This war of nerves brought yet another rule from the tough Quaker. Henceforth, all weapons would be left outside the agency building.

With the Koozers and Martin Kilgore safely back in white hands, Tatum extended the policy of withholding rations to prisoner negotiations as well.

> No one knew whether it would work well or not. But I thought it was right, and therefore the thing to do. In practice it worked grandly. I procured many captives of them afterwards without paying a dollar. That treatment made no inducement for them to obtain captives, while paying for them was an inducement.

To back his new regulations, Tatum went so far as to borrow troops from Grierson on issue day. While at the agency, they functioned as a civil police force. This was well within Quaker beliefs and did much to quiet the Indians, although it did not endear him to the members of the Friends Committee that oversaw the agencies.[13]

One man was unimpressed with Tatum or the soldiers. That was Satank. The old Koiet-senko was no longer "the white man's friend" as he had pledged at Medicine Lodge three years earlier. During the summer of 1870, his oldest and favorite son had raided into Texas with a group of young, overconfident warriors. As they approached a picket farmhouse, the settlers inside opened fire. Young Satank was mortally wounded. His companions fled in panic. After regaining their nerve, they returned for the body and hid it among some rocks.

---

[13]Tatum, *Red Brothers*, 35-48; Tatum to Patrick Field, September 19, 1870, reprinted in Austin *Weekly State Journal*, November 3, 1870. The Austin editor was under the impression that Mrs. Field had been captured the previous year. In fact she had been missing for six years.

By the time his father arrived to claim the body, scavengers had reduced it to a pile of bones. Old Satank was hysterical with grief, and his companions had to tie him up to prevent him from committing suicide. After calming down, he gathered the bones, washed them, and wrapped them in a new blanket. From that day on, he carried them wherever he went. On the trail, he led a pony with the bones carefully packed on it. In camp, he built a special lodge for the remains, and left food and water for the spirit. Now he lived only for revenge, hoping to die a warrior's death, taking as many whites as possible.[14]

Not long after the death of Young Satank, a Texan came to the agency to claim a mule that Old Satank was riding. Tatum called a hearing where the Texan was able to prove ownership by brands. Satank replied he had stolen the mule where his son had been killed, to compensate himself for the loss. He said he "loved it instead of his son" and ought to be allowed to keep it. When Tatum demanded the mule be returned, Satank suggested the agent accompany him outside for a fight to the death. The survivor would get the mule. Tatum refused, but got the mule back anyway. Another time Satank disrupted the ration issue until Tatum ran him off.[15]

As cold weather approached, the raiding season ended and the plains grew quiet. Meanwhile, in Austin, Governor Edmund Davis and the State Legislature groped for solutions to a problem they had helped create. A Reconstruction governor, Davis had been imposed on Texas by the state's military rulers. Once in office he had disbanded the Rangers, traditionally the frontier's first line of defense, establishing in their place a detested state police force to enforce federal edicts. Now his major concern was not Reconstruction but frontier defense, and he was desperate. Together with the legislature, he hammered out a bond issue to reestablish the Rangers. The

---

[14]Nye, *Carbine and Lance*, 113-14.
[15]Tatum, *Red Brothers*, 48-49.

Governor Edmund
J. Davis. *Texas State
Library and Archive.*

plan called for 550 mounted men in eleven companies posted throughout the frontier, to prepare for the next raiding season.

The proposal was attacked on all sides. The Indian Ring saw it as a threat to a very lucrative operation. Honest citizens distrusted Davis and viewed the plan as nothing more than an extension of his police force. Even so, the Ranger force was approved, although not in the form Davis intended; the War Department insisted it serve as a volunteer auxiliary to the army rather than as a permanent independent force. The federal government would provide subsistence while the state paid the salaries during the volunteers' terms of service.

Meanwhile, up at Fort Sill, the Indians settled in for the winter. And the people of Texas deluged the army with letters demanding military intervention.

Colonel Ranald S. Mackenzie. *National Archives*

Part 2: The Raid

CHAPTER 3
"I'll Bet Satanta is Going on a Raid"

Although the raids slackened during the winter, they began earlier than usual and with a new ferocity in 1871. "The entire border was ablaze," Lieutenant Robert Carter of the Fourth Cavalry recalled, "and the stories that these wretched settlers brought in from time to time of murder, rapine, burning, pillaging and plundering was almost heartrending."[1]

In its slow, methodical way, the military was doing what it could, but it was hamstrung by the Quaker Policy and by skepticism in its own ranks. Still, it took a step in the right direction by appointing Colonel Ranald S. Mackenzie to command the Fourth Cavalry. Only thirty years old, Mackenzie already had a distinguished career as a line officer. Graduating at the top of his class at West Point in 1862, he had gone straight into combat, first as an engineer, then as a cavalryman. His rise had been meteoric. Within three years, he had been breveted to brigadier general of the Union Army. General Grant called him "the most promising young officer in the army."[2] But Mackenzie had paid for his advancement. By the time he came to Texas, he had suffered six major wounds, some of them nearly fatal. He could neither walk nor ride any distance without great pain, and had two fingers missing from

---

[1]Carter, *On the Border*, 58.

[2]Grant, *Memoirs*, 2:541. Mackenzie's life is covered in Robinson, *Bad Hand*.

his right hand. He was foul-tempered and ambitious, and his men both respected and feared him.

After the war, Mackenzie was appointed colonel of the 41st Infantry, a black regiment comprised largely of undisciplined former slaves. Within two years, he had whipped it into one of the best regiments in the army. In February 1871, he took command of the Fourth Cavalry at Fort Concho in southwest Texas. After several weeks of rigorous training, the Fourth was sent north to Fort Richardson, in the center of the most heavily raided area. Headquarters and five companies marched out of Fort Concho on March 25, 1871. On April 7, they crossed the Salt Creek Prairie, only a few miles from their goal. On the western edge, they passed the graves of four black teamsters massacred in a Kiowa raid only two months earlier on January 24. One was Britt Johnson, the brave ex-slave who had ransomed the Young County captives. In all, Lieutenant Carter counted twenty-one graves that day. This stretch of prairie was the most dangerous place in Texas.[3]

This was the Texas that the Easterners failed to see. Yet the letters flooding army headquarters showed some sort of reassurance was needed on the frontier. In the spring of 1871, General Sherman, decided to personally inspect the frontier. Although he was as skeptical as anyone, his traveling companion, Inspector General Randolph Marcy, was more realistic. Marcy had served on the Texas frontier in the 1850s, and fully understood the Indians and their capacity for war. But it was Sherman, not Marcy, who had to be convinced. And there were those in Texas who actually hoped that "one of the numerous Indian depredations that are constantly occurring on our frontier might happen while General Sherman was in the country and close to the scene of destruction, so that he would be fully impressed with the

---

[3]Carter, *On the Border,* 69; Nye, *Carbine and Lance,* 123; Kellogg, *Journal,* 150.

General W.T. Sherman.
*Collection of C.M.
Robinson III*

great necessity of more efficient military operations to prevent them."[4]

After a quiet winter, the Kiowas and Comanches at Fort Sill were growing restless. With the arrival of spring, the time was right for raiding. Satank still carried the bones of his son, grieving over them with ever increasing hatred for the race he held responsible for his death. The annuity goods that the government was obligated to provide no later than October 15 of the previous year still had not arrived. The forays into Texas became "unusually frequent, and were marked by a degree of ferocity unknown during recent years."[5]

---

[4]*Army and Navy Journal*, 7:45 (June 10, 1871), 675.
[5]Myers to Editors of *The Nation*, April 30, 1871, manuscript copy in Myers Papers; "unusually frequent....", McConnell, *Five Years a Cavalryman*, 273.

On March 11, Tatum wrote the committee, "I think the Kiowa Indians are determined to provoke a war. They have killed several persons lately in Texas, and have stolen many horses." He believed that the Indians intended to raid then scatter, staying out of the way until fall, when they could draw their annuity goods.[6]

One day in April, Lieutenant Samuel L. Woodward, adjutant at Fort Sill, was writing at his desk when Satanta came in, looking for Colonel Grierson. As Woodward later related to Lieutenant Myers, Satanta put his hand on the adjutant's shoulder and demanded, "Where big Chief?"

"No sabe. Sit down," Woodward replied, pointing to a chair. "How?"

"No bueno," Satanta answered and sat. Woodward continued writing. After a lengthy silence, Satanta asked, "How long 'way, Big Chief?"

"Un poco tiempo. Mebby so. Little while be back. Take a cigar, Satanta."

The Kiowa reached for a cigar and Woodward resumed writing. He was so involved with his paperwork he almost forgot Satanta. Half an hour later he looked up and was alarmed by what he saw. Satanta, who normally enjoyed cigars, was not smoking it. Instead, he was unconsciously tearing it to pieces, his eyes riveted to the floor.

"Hello, Satanta!" Woodward said. "I'll send orderly. Mebby so find Big Chief. Hungry?"

"No. Mebby so squaw, papoose, heap hungry. Cold. Heap agua [i.e., rain]."

"Want chuck-a-way [bread]?" Woodward asked.

The chief grunted in assent.

Woodward wrote an order for the post baker to supply Satanta with several loaves of bread. He was getting uneasy.

---

[6]Tatum, *Red Brothers*, 107.

The normally arrogant and boastful Kiowa was sitting quietly, as though something was weighing heavily on his mind. He was armed while Woodward himself had no weapon at hand, and was thoroughly familiar with the Kiowa's reputation for bloodshed. They were completely alone, since the orderly had been sent out to look for Grierson. He tried to strike up a conversation, but the only language they had in common was an English-Spanish patois and a few hand signs. Eventually, Satanta left and Woodward went back to his paperwork.

Satanta's behavior was so unusual that when Grierson came in, Woodward mentioned it to him and wondered if the chief "might be meditating mischief." That night, as several of the officers discussed the possibility of an Indian outbreak, Woodward told them about the incident in the office and said, "I'll bet Satanta is going on a raid into Texas."[7]

There were many events during that spring. The Civilized Tribes met for their annual council in Okmulgee and passed a resolution calling for a conference with the Indians from the plains agencies. The purpose was to discuss mutual problems with whites and consider solutions that could be reached without bloodshed. Superintendent Enoch Hoag appointed a council for all the groups, which was to convene at the Wichita Agency on April 24. That day was rainy and no Indians came. The next day they began arriving. By Saturday, April 29, enough delegates were present to make preliminary arrangements, after which they adjourned until Monday. When they finally met, thirteen tribes were represented, among them the Comanche, Kiowa, Apache, Cheyenne and Arapaho. The moderate Kicking Bird attended on behalf of the Kiowas.[8]

While the Indians conferred, Sherman and his party were

---

[7]Myers, Papers.
[8]Tatum, *Red Brothers*, 108-11.

at departmental headquarters in San Antonio, preparing for their departure for West Texas. The party left San Antonio on May 2. The early part of the trip was uneventful. Then, on May 7, between Menard and Fort McKavett, Sherman encountered "three armed men, who said three Indians had that morning run off twenty-five horses before their eyes. They were going to the rear and looked excited." Thus far, however, it had been the only sign of Indians, and there is no indication that Sherman was unduly concerned.[9]

On the North Fork of the Red River, there was yet another gathering of fighting men, and another conference. This one, however, was a war council. Perhaps as many as 150 Kiowas, Kiowa-Apaches and Comanches had accepted an invitation to come, smoke the war pipe and discuss a major raid into Texas. Among them were Satanta, old Satank, Eagle Heart, and a bold teen-aged sub-chief named Big Tree who already had a reputation for ferocity.[10]

But the most important figure present was Maman-ti or Sky-Walker. He was the do-ha-te, the medicine man, an owl prophet who could predict the future by communicating with animals. Although his magic gave him the power of life and death, he was not a dreaded figure to his own people. In fact, his position in the Kiowa community was much like that of an Irish priest or a rabbi in a modern society. He was wise, kind and generous. Like most plains medicine men, he was undoubtedly responsible for the education of the children and served as their role model. All the same, he probably was the

---

[9]Marcy, Journal, in Rister, "Documents," *Panhandle-Plains Historical Review.* 9: 14-16.

[10]Nye, *Carbine and Lance,* 126-27. Nye was stationed at Fort Sill in the 1930s and got the Indian version of the Warren Wagon Train Massacre largely from Yellow Wolf, the last survivor. He supplemented that with information from friends and relatives of Indians who had participated. Among them was George Hunt, a Kiowa, who had heard it from Big Tree. Ida Lasater Huckabay (*Ninety-Four Years in Jack County*) got the story from Hunt, who visited Jacksboro in 1938. Any story of the Indian side of the massacre is based almost exclusively on accounts by Nye and Mrs. Huckabay.

Big Tree, a Kiowa
arrested for the raid.
*Archives & Manuscripts
Division of the Oklahoma
Historical Society.*

most powerful Kiowa since Dohasen, a wily and gifted war
chief who was the moving force behind the tribe's raids into
Texas. Maman-ti was personally responsible for the massacre
of Britt Johnson and his companions that January.[11]

As Sherman moved west on his inspection tour, this powerful Indian force moved south, crossing the Red River between
what are now Vernon and Electra. They established a base
camp by the river, which they called Skunk Headquarters
because of the large numbers of that animal in the area. Here
they stripped down to the essentials necessary for a lightning

---

[11]Nye, *Carbine and Lance*, 127; Mayhall, *Kiowas*, 144.

raid. Saddles, blankets and other heavy gear were cached. Spare ponies were hobbled and several young boys were told off to guard the camp. Extra bridles and lariats were packed because the Indians expected to return with a large number of stolen horses and mules. The warriors who were to handle the stolen stock left their own ponies at the camp, and either rode double or grabbed a horse's tail and trotted alongside. With everything in readiness, Maman-ti led his warriors south into the Texas interior. At the same time, Sherman was heading north toward Fort Griffin. This post was the last stop before Fort Richardson. Between the two forts lay the deadly Salt Creek Prairie. Soldier and Indian would have to cross it.

Not far from the Salt Creek Prairie, citizens of Jacksboro had prepared a petition in anticipation of Sherman's visit. Signed by W.M. McConnell and H. Horton "in behalf of the Citizens of Jack Co[unty]," it asked Sherman to investigate "the many and cruel murders and outrages that have been perpetrated against our peaceful citizens and neighbors...we do most earnestly pray for some *immediate* relief, that we may feel a comparative safety in our lives and some protection and security in the possession of our property..."

It went on to list 129 Indian-related deaths in Jack County from August 1859 through April 1871. Of these, twelve were from January through April 1871, alone.

"In addition to the above great sacrifice of life," the petition continued, "hundreds have been driven from their houses through fear and more than two thousand head of Horses stolen from the citizens of the county.

"Losses of Cattle and destruction of out buildings with severity felt in their loss, have not been ennumerated [*sic*] in this account.

"Taking into consideration the smallness of our population (at no time exceeding six hundred) and so fearful destruction of

58

life and property [this] is the only argument needed to show our want of protection, to which end we earnestly and respectfully ask your co-operation in our behalf," the petition concluded.[12]

Sherman's party reached Fort Griffin on May 14, and made camp near the post. The following day was spent on routine inspection. Aside from living conditions, which were deplorable, and the questionable legal status of the government's occupation of the military reservation itself, Marcy found nothing worth noting in his journal. But at the same time two scouting parties from Fort Griffin, one of Rangers with Tonkawa Indian guides, and the other of regular cavalry and Tonkawas, were out chasing hostiles and so missed the commanding general's visit altogether.[13]

On May 16, Sherman left Griffin. Although he declined a stronger escort to accompany him to Fort Richardson, there is some evidence the local commanders were taking no chances in an area they knew was dangerous. Six days earlier, a cavalry unit consisting of one officer and twenty-five enlisted men had left Fort Richardson "to scout between Forts Richardson and Griffin." And some detachments of Company "B" of the Fourth Cavalry did not arrive from Fort Concho until May 18, even though the rest of the company had arrived May 6.[14] It was unusual for individual companies to be broken down into detachments during a regimental transfer, and there is no official explanation as to why one part of Company "B" arrived twelve days later than the other. Thus there is a strong possibility that Sherman was shadowed by soldiers throughout his tour of the region.

---

[12]Citizens to Sherman, May 2, 1871, original document reproduced in facsimile in Hamilton, *Sentinel,* 237-43.

[13]Marcy, Journal, *Panhandle-Plains Historical Review,* 9: 17-18; Post Medical Report, Fort Griffin, Texas, May 1871.

[14]Post Medical Report, Fort Griffin, Texas, May 1871; Post Returns, Fort Richardson, Texas, May 1871.

Sherman's party camped the night of the sixteenth at the
abandoned post of Fort Belknap in Young County. Marcy
noted, "The Indians come here often, and as there has of late
been no picket left here, they have troubled travelers and the
two or three families that live here a good deal." Sherman
ordered a picket be sent from Richardson.[15]

In the Kiowa camp, Maman-ti was making medicine. He
sat apart from the others, who were grouped together in
silence waiting for some message to the do-ha-te from a dead
ancestor. Soon they heard the cry of an owl and the soft beat
of his wings. The Do-ha-te stood, raised his arms and
repeated what the owl had told him.

"Two parties of Tehannas will pass....The first will be a
small party. Perhaps we could overcome it easily. Many of you
will be eager to do so. But it must not be attacked. The medicine forbids. Later...another party will come. This one may be
attacked. The attack will be successful."

The following morning the Indians entered Young County,
heading for the Butterfield Trail where it crossed Salt Creek
Prairie between Fort Belknap and Fort Richardson. This was
the spot where Carter had counted the twenty-one graves. It
was a favorite ambush spot since it was lonely, but well-trav-
eled. With or without Maman-ti's oracle, the Kiowas knew
they eventually would have some quarry. It was simply a matter of waiting.[16]

Sherman left camp at Fort Belknap at 6 a.m. that day.
Meanwhile, at Fort Richardson, Lieutenant Carter was

---

[15]Post Medical Report, Fort Griffin, Texas, May 1871; Marcy Journal, *Panhandle-Plains
Historical Review.* 9: 18.

[16]Nye, *Carbine and Lance,* 127-28. Nye and other writers have generally placed Sherman's
passage and the Warren Wagon Train Massacre the same day. Much of this apparently is
based on recollections of both Kiowas and whites many years later. However, examination of
contemporary records, including Marcy's journal, post returns for Fort Richardson, and military correspondence, shows Sherman crossed the Salt Creek Prairie on May 17, arriving at
Richardson that evening, while the Warren massacre occurred the following morning.

ordered to select fifteen men and ride up the road to meet Sherman and escort him into the post. Two gun crews were to prepare a salute with a couple of three-inchers that happened to be at Richardson. Carter went through company after company looking for gunners, until he found a sergeant and a corporal who had served in the artillery. As these two began drilling crews to work the guns, Carter rode out of the post toward Rock Station on the Fort Griffin Road, with fifteen men, four mules he was to offer as fresh exchanges for Sherman's ambulance, and instructions to offer Mackenzie's quarters to the commanding general.[17]

As Sherman's party moved toward Fort Richardson, Marcy was struck by the Indian devastation. "The remains of several ranches were observed today, the occupants of which have been either killed or driven off to the more dense settlements by the Indians," he wrote. "Indeed, this rich and beautiful section does not contain today so many white people as it did when I visited it eighteen years ago, and if the Indian marauders are not punished, the whole country seems to be in a fair way of becoming totally depopulated."[18]

The party continued across the Salt Creek Prairie. The Indians were already there, and had been in position since daybreak, on a sandstone hill that give them a good view over a long stretch of the road. Flint Creek ran along the foot of the hill, lined by a few trees. From there, the prairie was open and flat for several miles until another hill called Cox Mountain, there the timbered area began. Between the two heights there was almost no cover except for a mesquite tree here and there. Anyone caught in the middle of the prairie would be completely exposed with no place to go. About noon, the Kiowa scouts saw some movement on the road at the west end of the

[17]Carter, *On the Border,* 75-76.
[18]Marcy, Journal, *Panhandle-Plains Historical Review,* 9: 18-19.

prairie. This was reported back to the main war party, and there was a lot of excited whispering. Some of the warriors wanted to attack, but Maman-ti quieted them down as he watched the strangers move closer. Soon, he recognized a vehicle escorted by a group of outriders. This was the first group seen in the prophecy. It was to be left alone. Perhaps, also, Maman-ti considered the fact that military transports always had heavily armed outriders, and these strangers appeared well disciplined and capable of inflicting heavy losses on any attacker.[19]

Sherman rode on, unaware of how close he had come to death. The man who had devastated Georgia and South Carolina was in a particularly good mood when he reached Rock Station. After accepting a salute by the mounted escort from Fort Richardson, he greeted Carter like a "long lost brother" and introduced him to Marcy and other members of his staff. He declined the offer of the mules, saying his were reasonably fresh and fast.

As for quarters, Sherman replied, "That is kind in Mackenzie to tender the use of his quarters, but I have got plenty of canvas and we will pitch our tents right behind and close to him. Your horses look warm. It would be too hard on them to try and keep up with us. If you will put us on the right road, you had better come in at your leisure. I appreciate it just as much, and I will thank Mackenzie personally for his kindness in sending you and such a fine looking detachment out to insure my safety."

Carter was not particularly happy to hear the general's praise. His mind was on the work that had gone into putting together and drilling two gun crews. There was no way now to notify the gunners of the change and have them ready in time to fire the salute. As it turned out, Sherman rode into Fort

---

[19]Nye, *Carbine and Lance*, 128.

Richardson unannounced, the gun crews were caught unaware, and the salute was never fired.

Among those awaiting his arrival was a delegation composed of McConnell, one of the signers of the petition for relief, W.W. Duke, R.J. Winders, J.R. Robinson, Peter Hart and General H.H. Gaines, all citizens of Jacksboro. Each had his own story of robbery and murder. They detailed their livestock losses and wanted help recovering them. Finally, to emphasize their point, they showed several white scalps, some female, which they said had been recovered from Kiowas and Comanches who were known to be reservation Indians.

Sherman listened politely, but shook his head to indicate he still had not seen enough evidence to convince him that the problem was really serious. He assured the citizens that when he reached Fort Sill, he would investigate charges that the Indians were receiving guns and ammunition from the post, and were allowed to bring stolen stock into the reservation. The delegation left feeling the effort had been futile and that their situation was hopeless. Meanwhile, Sherman went around Fort Richardson visiting with old sergeants and talking with the men. He also stopped by the houses to chat with wives and children, congratulating them for sharing the isolation of frontier duty. As if to emphasize the point, he suggested that officers should marry while still young. If the citizens of Jacksboro felt abandoned, the soldiers and their families were convinced the commanding general had their best interests at heart.[20]

---

[20]Carter, *On the Border*, 76-80; Huckabay, *Ninety-four Years*, 167-68.

CHAPTER 4

"They Intend to Continue Their Atrocities in Texas"

While Sherman relaxed at Fort Richardson, Maman-ti was having trouble with some of his warriors. No Kiowa was legally or morally bound to cooperate with the group if he decided his own interests were elsewhere. And several members of the party were ready to leave the main band and strike out on their own. But somehow, perhaps by force of personality or by threat of the supernatural, the Do-ha-te was able to hold them together. May 18 dawned and still the Indians waited. Finally they saw a wagon train approaching the prairie from the east. There were ten wagons in all, loaded with corn for Fort Griffin, under a contract between the government and Captain Henry Warren, a freighter from Weatherford. The train was run by wagonmaster Nathan S. Long.

The Indians watched with growing excitement as the wagons rounded the north end of Cox Mountain and came out onto the prairie. Maman-ti managed to hold them back until the train reached the middle of the prairie where there was no cover. Then he motioned to Satanta, who raised his bugle to signal the charge. Whether Satanta ever got off a note will never be known. Before he could blow, the warriors were charging down the slope. Neither Yellow Wolf nor Big Tree, two of the participants, remembered a bugle call that day, but Big Tree recalled hearing an eagle bone whistle that the Indians always carried. Whipped into a frenzy by the long wait, by their own yelling and by the shrill sound of the whistle, the Indians raced to see who would strike the first coup. That physical contact with a fighting enemy—even if it was only a touch—counted most of all.

Yellow Wolf was in the lead. He had the fastest pony, along with a reckless courage that bordered on foolhardiness. Big Tree was close behind. The rest of the band scattered across the prairie, with the warriors on foot and on the slower ponies trailing in the rear.

The teamsters saw them as they tore out of the trees along Flint Creek. Long ordered the wagons corralled. Hurriedly, the whites turned off the road and began forming into a circle, but Yellow Wolf charged in front of the last wagon, cutting it off before the corral was complete. The teamsters had their rifles out and were diving to the ground. They were no tenderfeet. They knew how to fight. By now, though, the Indians were in the middle of the broken corral. Big Tree made the first coup, Yellow Wolf, the second, with two Kiowa-Apaches claiming the third and fourth. After the fourth, coups didn't count for much and fighting became general. Dust and smoke began to cloud the area. Or-dlee, a Comanche, jumped off his horse and dashed over to fight one of the whites hand-to-hand. Someone fired and he died instantly. Red Warbonnet, a Kiowa chief, received a severe wound in his thigh. Although at least three of the teamsters had died in the first rush, the others were firing rapidly and accurately.

The Indians pulled away from the corral and began running the classic circle around the wagons. In his second time around, Yellow Wolf found another warrior, Tson-to-goodle, wounded in the leg. Two other Indians dragged him away. Storm clouds were gathering in the sky, with the sun trying to shine out from behind them. The wagons were obscured by a pall of dust and smoke. Off to the west, two women who had accompanied the party encouraged the warriors with shrill tongue-rattling.

There was an opening on the east side of the circle of Indians. Seven teamsters broke through it on foot, in a mad dash toward the trees by Cox Mountain. Yellow Wolf saw them, rounded up several warriors and started in pursuit. One man was shot down on the prairie, but the others kept on. A second white was killed at the edge of the timber. The Indians broke off the chase and rode back to the wagons. The sky was growing black and they were anxious to divide the plunder and be on their way before the storm broke.

The corral of wagons had grown quiet now, but the Indians were cautious. It didn't seem possible to them that everyone inside was dead. No one had paid attention to the killing after the initial coups. They continued a careful circle around the wagons, noting the positions of the white bodies and trying to reconcile them with each warrior's individual count. Finally, Hau-tau, an eager young warrior on his first raid, started toward one of the wagons. Then he stopped and retreated a few steps. Not a sound came from the wagon. He started forward again. White Horse and Set-maunte, older and more experienced warriors, grabbed him and tried to hold him back. He broke away from them, ran to a second wagon, touched it and shouted, "I claim the wagon and all that is in it!" Instantly, a wounded teamster, probably Samuel Elliott, threw back his canvass cover and blasted Hau-tau in the face with his rifle.

White Horse and Set-maunte had started rounding up their claim of the mules when they heard the shot. They rushed over and found Hau-tau on the ground, still breathing, his face torn up by the heavy caliber bullet. Enraged by the shooting, the Indians began tearing the wagon train to pieces. Recalling the massacre decades later, the survivors would not elaborate on what they did with the bodies, or with the wounded teamster who had shot Hau-tau, but the conclusions can be drawn by the reports of the soldiers who found them. The Indians did say they set fire to the wagons and contents, and returned to the hill with the captured mules. They placed Or-dlee's body in a crevice on the south side of the hill and covered it with rocks. By then, the rain was falling in torrents. They tied their wounded to horses and began the slow journey back to Fort Sill.[1]

Late that night, as the troopers at Fort Richardson were feeding the horses, two men appeared at the stables. One of them, Thomas Brazeal, was badly wounded.

"We are teamsters from Warren's wagon train which was attacked yesterday...by about one hundred Indians on Salt Creek Prairie," Brazeal explained. "Seven of our men were killed—four men and myself escaped—all are wounded but my wounds are the most serious."

Brazeal had a gunshot wound and an arrow wound in his foot, and was weak from the loss of blood. His companions had carried him to a nearby ranch, where they had secured horses for the dash into Fort Richardson.[2]

The wounded teamster was taken to the hospital and put to bed. Sherman was informed and came to hear the story for himself. The commanding general was thunderstruck. The massacre scene was only about four miles from Rock Station, where he had declined Carter's escort. There were even those among the troops who thought he had been the intended victim. He reacted immediately. Carter was summoned to take down and dispatch a flurry of orders.[3] Mackenzie was to go to the massacre site and report on what he found, then follow the trail of the Indians. Colonel William H. Wood, 11th Infantry and commander at Fort Griffin, was ordered to send all his

---

[1]Myers, Papers; Nye, *Carbine and Lance*, 128-31; Huckabay, *Ninety-four Years*, 170-72.
[2]Huckabay, *Ninety-four Years*, 168.
[3]Carter, *On the Border*, 80.

available cavalry to rendezvous with Mackenzie's force at the head of the Little Wichita.

Sherman also had a second meeting with citizens from Jack and Parker counties. This time, he was in a much better frame of mind to listen, although, officially, his hands were still tied. "As these Indians are in the care and custody of the Indian Department," he wrote, "I explained to these citizens my inability to apply a remedy, and advised them to come with me to Fort Sill and confer with the agent Mr. Tatum." He also accepted a petition with affidavits, in which the citizens charged "all, or nearly all these depredations to the Indians of this [Fort Sill] Reservation." He personally forwarded the petition to the War Department in Washington.[4]

In Sherman's mind, there was no question as to where the blame actually belonged.

> I do think the people of Texas have a right to complain, only their complaints are now against the troops who are powerless, but should be against the Department that feeds and harbors these Indians when their hands are yet red with blood.[5]

By this, of course, he meant the Department of Interior and its Indian Bureau.

Although he deferred to the rules when conferring with civilians, Sherman had plans of his own for the Indians responsible for this particular massacre. He told Mackenzie:

> As you are on the point of starting for the Indians who yesterday attacked the corn train...and as, in their pursuit, you may have to enter what is Known as the Fort Sill Reservation, I hereby authorize you to enter said Reservation, and if the trail be fresh, and you should overtake the party anywhere within thirty or forty miles of Red River, you will not hesitate to attack the party, secure the prop-

---

[4]Sherman to General E.D. Townsend, May 24, 1871, in RG 94 1305 AGO 1871, Letters Received, Main Series, 1871-1880, hereinafter referred to as Letters Received; Marcy, Journal, *Panhandle-Plains Historical Review*, 9:19.

[5]Sherman to Townsend, May 24, 1871, Letters Received.

erty stolen, and any other property or stock in their possession, and bring them to me at Fort Sill.

Should the trail scatter, and yet in your opinion, lead into said Reservation, you may in like manner come to Fort Sill, that we may, through the Indian Agent there, recover the stolen stock and get possession of the party of Indians who attacked this train and killed the seven (7) men as reported.[6]

The fact that troops could not legally enter an Indian reservation without the agent's permission was of no particular interest to Sherman. He meant to have these Indians, and he was not overly concerned about the fine points of agency rights. In his instructions to Colonel Wood, he said:

It is all important that this case be followed up with extreme vigor, and principally that we find out whether or not, the impression be well founded that the numerous robberies and murders on this Frontier have been done by the Fort Sill Reservation Indians.[7]

Rain was still pouring when Mackenzie rode out toward the massacre scene. By now, several inches of water covered the parade ground at Fort Richardson. The six companies of cavalry had to wade through swollen streams and became bogged in mud. Often they had to dismount and lead their horses.[8]

These scene at the wagon train was sickening. Dr. J.H. Patzki, post surgeon, was professional in his report, stating:

All the bodies were riddled with bullets, covered with gashes, and the skulls crushed, evidently with an axe found bloody on the place; some of the bodies exhibited also signs of having been stabbed with arrows. One of the bodies was even more mutilated than the others, it having been found fastened with a chain to the pole of a wagon lying over a fire with the face to the ground, the tongue being cut out. Owing to the charred condition of the soft parts it was impossible to determine whether the man was burned before or after his death. The scalps of all but one were taken.[9]

---

[6]Sherman to Mackenzie, May 19, 1871, ibid.   [7]Sherman to Wood, May 19, 1871, ibid.
[8]Carter, *On the Border*, 81, and Carter, *Old Sergeant's Story*, 679-70.
[9]Dr. Patzki's letter has been reprinted many times. This particular quotation is from Nye, *Carbine and Lance*, 131. The one man who had not been scalped was bald.

There is little doubt that the charred teamster, Samuel Elliott, had been roasted alive. Had he been dead, the Indians would not have bothered.

Only five bodies were found at the train. The other two, who had been killed while fleeing, were located on the prairie. Forty-one mules had been taken by the Indians. The bodies of the rest were found nearby, where they Indians had killed them. The corn sacks had been cut open, and the contents had been piled up in heaps, along with harnesses and other paraphernalia. In addition to Samuel Elliott, the dead were identified as wagonmaster Nathan Long, N.J. Baxter, James Bowman, James Elliott, James Williams and John Mullen.[10]

The next morning, Sergeant Miles Varily took a burial detail out to the site. The ground was saturated from the rain. A large pit was dug, and the soldiers repeatedly had to bail out the water in order to continue working. The victims were laid out in the bed of a wagon, which was lowered into the grave. After it was filled in, the troopers placed two stones over it, with seven marks cut in them.[11]

Sherman left Fort Richardson on May 20. He was cheerful and talkative, giving no visible indication that anything was out of the ordinary. As his ambulance started to move out with its infantry escort, someone remarked that his scalp might be in danger.

"Oh no," the general smiled as he patted the Winchester rifle in his lap. "I have sixteen shots here myself."[12]

The same day, Mackenzie was held up by high water on the south bank of the Little Wichita. The rain had obliterated the trail and now he was on his way to Fort Sill. Farther north, the Indians were crossing the Big Wichita, using boats made from willow branches and covered with canvas. With their guns, plunder and wounded inside, they swam alongside and pushed

---

[10]Carter, *On the Border*, 80-81.
[11]Huckabay, *Ninety-four Years*, 169.
[12]Carter, *On the Border*, 83-84.

them across the river. Quitan and Tomasi, two Mexicans who had been adopted into the tribe as captives, saw a herd of buffalo coming in from the west and swimming the river. Since they prided themselves on their hunting prowess, they took two Kiowas and stayed behind, and killed between twelve and fifteen of the animals. As they were butchering the carcasses, they were surprised by Lieutenant Peter Martin Boehm's twenty-five-man scout, that had left Fort Richardson on May 10, and was now en route back to the post. In the ensuing fight, Tomasi and his horse were killed, and one soldier and two horses were slightly wounded. The other three hostiles dove into the river and swam among the buffalo to escape. Ahead, the main band of Indians heard the shots and fled. When Quitan and the two Kiowas finally caught up, they all continued northward.

Back at the ford, Boehm ordered a search of the vicinity. His men found tracks that convinced him that all captured stock was being run through the Big Wichita area, between the head of the Brazos and the Red River. The soldiers took Tomasi's scalp, which Boehm gave to Carter back at Fort Richardson.

Meanwhile, the raiders had crossed the Red River and reached their village on the reservation where Maman-ti, always a shadowy figure when whites were concerned, seems to have disappeared from view. The arrival home was too late for the wounded Hau-tau. Screwworms had entered his wound and reached the brain. He died a few days later.[13]

Unaware of events in Texas, the Civilized Tribes had held their council with the Plains Indians at the Wichita Agency. Lawrie Tatum attended with Kicking Bird. Although the grievances were many, most of the delegates spoke for peace.

---

[13]Nye, *Carbine and Lance*, 132; Major J.K. Mizner to AAG, Department of Texas, June 11, 1871, Letters Received.

At the urging of some, the literate Cherokees agreed to publish the speeches and complaints in their newspaper which, presumably, would be sent to Washington. The Kiowas had remained unusually quiet, letting the other tribes have the floor. Finally, Kicking Bird spoke.

"I like the talk," he said, "but cannot promise to accept it all at this time, but may in the future. You have often heard that the Kiowas were a bad and foolish people, which is true. The reason is our land has been taken from us, and we are not permitted to purchase ammunition. If you wish us to become a good people you must get Washington to do something for us, especially in furnishing us with guns and ammunition."

To Tatum, this meant there was unrest and dissention in the Kiowa ranks. On May 22, he wrote his committee:

> I think the Indians do not intend to commit depredations here this summer, but from their actions and sayings they intend to continue their atrocities in Texas. I believe affairs will continue to get worse until there is a different course pursued with the Indians. I know of no reason why they should not be treated the same as white people for the same offence. It is not right to be feeding and clothing them, and let them raid with impunity in Texas. *Will the committee sustain me in having Indians arrested for murder, and turned over to the proper authorities of Texas for trial?* [italics added][14]

At that moment, the question was hypothetical. Tatum could not have known that within a couple of days, he would be forced to make just such a decision.

---

[14]Tatum, *Red Brothers*, 113-16.

Chief Lone Wolf, a paramount Kiowa leader.
*Archives & Manuscripts Division of
the Oklahoma Historical Society.*

Part 3: The Arrest

CHAPTER 5
"You and I Are Going to Die Right Here"

On Tuesday, May 23, only a day after he wrote his committee, Tatum received a visit from the general-in-chief. Sherman told him about the massacre in Texas, and asked if he knew of any Indians who had "gone to Texas lately." Tatum replied that he thought he would find out within a few days, since it was nearly time for them to draw rations.[1] He also told Sherman that the Kiowas and Comanches were "beyond his control, that they come and go as they please, and he was not at all surprised to hear that they were a hundred miles off, killing citizens engaged in their usual business, and stealing horses, and mules."

They had a long conversation, and Sherman came away convinced that the agent was a "good, honest man."

The next day, they talked again. Tatum said not a single Kiowa or Comanche child was attending the agency school. Likewise, efforts to convert the tribes to agriculture had failed although the Indians had now been on the agency for two years. "Their progress in Civilization is a farce," Sherman remarked after the meeting.[2]

In his investigation, Sherman determined that Satanta was missing, and probably was with the war party that attacked

[1]Tatum, *Red Brothers*, 116.
[2]Sherman to Townsend, May 24, 1871, Letters Received.

75

the wagon train. "I hope that Genl. McKenzie will track him to his camp," he wrote. "Meanwhile I advise that the Indian Agent here be instructed to issue supplies only to Indians present, that when there is proof of murder and robbery, the actual perpetrators be surrendered to the Governor of Texas for trial and punishment. A few examples would have a salutory [*sic*] effect."[3]

Looking back over his trip so far, particularly in light of the recent events around Fort Richardson, Sherman concluded the military policy should be one of expansion and subjugation rather than containment, and that forts should be at the vanguard of the frontier. As it was, an erratic line meandered from Fort McKavett in the south, to Fort Concho in the far west, northeast to Fort Griffin, still farther eastward to Fort Richardson, then northward to Fort Sill. He felt McKavett and Concho were ideally suited for the purpose, but that Griffin and Richardson "are not well placed unless we are willing to retreat as it were before the Indians." Instead, he preferred reactivating Camp Cooper, an antebellum post west of Fort Griffin, and establishing a post near the head of the Little Wichita. This would make a tight line curving southwestward from Sill to McKavett. As for the immediate situation, he ordered Brigadier General John Pope, commanding the Department of the Missouri, of which Fort Sill was a part, to release companies of Grierson's Tenth Cavalry then posted to Fort Dodge, Kansas, and Camp Supply, Indian Territory, and place them under Grierson's immediate jurisdiction. These troops would be used to seal the area south of the reservation by strengthening an existing picket at Cache Creek and reactivating old Camp Radziminski. The Indians "would find it more difficult to get out, and still more so, to get back to the Reservation with their herds of stolen stock," Sherman said.[4]

---

[3]Ibid. Sherman consistently misspelled Mackenzie's name.   [4]Ibid.

CHAPTER 5: "YOU AND I ARE GOING TO DIE..."

Grierson got his troops, but Sherman failed in his efforts to
tighten the line of forts. Nothing was ever done to regarrison
Camp Cooper or establish a permanent post at the Little
Wichita. Fort Griffin and Fort Richardson continued to func-
tion until long after the Indian Wars in Texas had ended.

On Friday, the Indians came to get their rations. Satanta,
Satank, Eagle Heart and Big Tree went into Tatum's office,
where Satanta told the agent he had come to make a "big
speech."

"I have heard that you have stolen a large portion of our
annuity goods and given them to the Texans," he began. "I
have repeatedly asked you for arms and ammunition, which
you have not furnished, and made many other requests which
have not been granted. You do not listen to my talk. The white
people are preparing to build a railroad through our country,
which will not be permitted. Some years ago, we were taken
by the hair and pulled here close to the Texans where we have
to fight. But we have cut that loose now and are all going with
the Cheyennes to the Antelope Hills. When Gen. Custer was
here two or three years ago, he arrested me and kept me in
confinement several days.[5] But arresting Indians is played out
now and is never to be repeated. On account of these grievances, I took a short time ago about one hundred of my warriors, with the Chiefs Satank, Eagle Heart, Big Tree, Big Bow
and Fast Bear, and went to Texas, where we captured a train
not far from Fort Richardson, killed seven of the men, and
drove off about forty-one mules."

At this point, Satank broke in, and ordered Satanta in
Kiowa not to give any more names.

Continuing, Satanta said, "Three of my men were killed,

[5]Satanta and Lone Wolf had been arrested and placed in close confinement for several
weeks during General Philip H. Sheridan's winter campaign of 1868-69. Lieutenant Colonel
George Armstrong Custer had immediate responsibility for them and he and Satanta got to
know each other well.

77

but we are willing to call it even. If any other Indian comes here and claimed the honor of leading the party he will be lying to you, for I did it myself."

Satank, Big Tree and Eagle Heart all nodded assent.[6]

Tatum was thoroughly convinced that Satanta was telling the truth. He also believed that if he let it pass, he would be an accessory to the crime. But the situation was touchy and he couldn't handle it alone. He told his staff to go ahead with the issue, while he went to the fort. When he arrived at Colonel Grierson's quarters, Tatum said he wanted Satanta, Big Tree, Eagle Heart, Big Bow and Fast Bear arrested for murder. It was decided that the best course would be to bring the chiefs to the post, so they could be arrested under military jurisdiction. A message was sent to the agency ordering them to appear. Meanwhile, a unit of cavalry was mounted and ready, concealed behind the stone walls of the corral. Some fifteen or so soldiers were placed behind shutters in rooms fronting the porch of Grierson's house. Several officers and civilians were placed in key spots to cut off any escape. Women and children were ordered inside their houses. The entire area around officers' row was cleared.

As these orders were being carried out, Satanta strutted up, accompanied by Satank and nineteen or twenty other Kiowas, as well as Horace Jones, the post interpreter. Satanta said he had heard a big chief from Washington was at Fort Sill and indicated he had come to size him up. But when he saw the soldiers moving about the parade ground in front of the houses, he knew something unusual was happening and started for his horse. Grierson's orderly pulled a pistol and told him to sit down. "From that moment, he was a prisoner," Sherman observed.

---

[6]Tatum to Jonathan Richards, May 30, 1871, in Kiowa Agency, Federal, State and Local Court Relations, Trial of Satanta and Big Tree, Indian Archives Division, Oklahoma Historical Society, hereinafter cited as Kiowa file; Tatum to Hoag, extract in Nye, *Carbine and Lance*, 135; Sherman to Lieutenant General P.H. Sheridan, May 29, 1871, Letters Received.

Sherman himself sat down on the porch with Grierson, Marcy and several other officers, facing Satanta. Stumbling Bear and Kicking Bird appeared. The latter was well liked, and some of the officers shook hands with him and slapped him on the back. Satanta started down the steps to meet them, but several soldiers forced him back up to the porch at bayonet point. The general-in-chief was growing impatient. He ordered Kicking Bird back to the camps to tell the other chiefs to hurry.

"Let me go," Satanta demanded.

"No, Satanta will not leave!" Sherman snapped.

As Kicking Bird started to leave, Satanta called out to him, "Tell everybody to come."

"I notice that when you stepped off the porch, the soldiers started to use their guns on you," Stumbling Bear told Satanta. "What's the matter?"

"They aren't treating me right," he replied.

When the group assembled, Sherman demanded to know who was involved in the Warren Wagon Train Massacre. Satanta said he was, and began to recount the fight. But as he talked he began to suspect that these whites were not impressed. So he denied any involvement in the burning of Elliott. Even so, his version was much the same as the one Sherman had heard from the teamster Brazeal.

"And now, what are you going to do about it? Satanta demanded.[7]

Sherman replied that he, Satank, Big Tree and Eagle Heart (whom Sherman called Black Eagle) were under arrest and would be returned to Texas for trial. The Indians all knew this meant execution by hanging, a death unthinkable for a warrior. Satanta immediately changed his story. According to Marcy, he said "that although he was present at the fight, he

---

[7]Tatum, *Red Brothers*, 116-17; Nye, *Carbine and Lance*, 136-38; Myers, Papers; *Army and Navy Journal*, July 1, 1871, 735; Sherman to Sheridan, May 29, 1871, Letters Received.

did not kill anybody himself, neither did he blow his bugle....His young men wanted to have a little fight and to take a few white scalps, and he was prevailed upon to go with them merely to show them how to make war, but that he stood back during the engagement and merely gave directions."

Sherman called him a coward for leading warriors in an attack against teamsters who were not trained to fight. He added that any time Satanta wanted a fight on equal terms, the soldiers would oblige.[8]

As the men argued, two Kiowa women wandered into Grierson's quarters and found the front rooms full of black soldiers from his Tenth Cavalry. They tried to break out but were surrounded by armed troopers.

Meanwhile, on the porch, Satanta had gone into a rage. He threw back his blanket and went for his revolver. The shutters flew open and a dozen or more soldiers of the Tenth levelled their carbines at the Indians. Satanta calmed down.

About this point, someone noticed Big Tree was missing. He had stopped off at the post trader's store on his way to the meeting. The adjutant, Lieutenant Woodward, and Lieutenant Richard Pratt were sent with a company of cavalry to get him.

The trader's store was built on a height, level on the front and sides, with the ground sloping down from the rear. The trader had fenced the slope and used it as his vegetable patch. Pratt placed men to cover the front and sides of the building while Woodward took a detail inside. They found Big Tree behind the counter handing out goods. When he saw them, he dove through the glass rear window, hit the ground running and took off down the slope. Pratt sent his horsemen along the sides of the fence to head him off. As Big Tree ran, the gardener took a shot at him with a long rifle, and he

---

[8]Marcy, quoted in Wilbarger, *Indian Depredations*, 558.

stopped in his tracks. Glancing around, he saw his position was hopeless, and walked over and surrendered to the soldiers, who marched him to Grierson's porch.

By now, Kicking Bird was back with the important chiefs and warriors, who were hemmed onto the parade ground by cavalry. The troopers had streamed out of the corral at the sound of a bugle, cutting off all escape for the Indians in the quadrangle. Their options were to submit quietly or die as warriors. They, themselves, were not certain what they should do. Stumbling Bear was convinced the soldiers planned to kill them all. They swayed back and forth, wailing for their chiefs.

About this time, another party of Indians approached. When they saw what was happening, they made a break. Several cavalrymen gave chase and shooting erupted. One Indian was killed and another was mortally wounded. Private Edward Givens received a flesh wound in the leg with an arrow.

The shots alerted Eagle Heart who, like Big Tree, was arriving late. Knowing it meant trouble, he escaped. The shooting also frightened a group of Kiowa women and children camped near the commissary. They fled, some riding two to a pony, and within minutes their camp was completely deserted.[9]

---

[9]There are probably as many different versions of the arrest as there were people present. Nye *(Carbine and Lance,* 137-42) gives the most detailed account, which came largely from interviews with various Kiowas, particularly Andrew Stumbling Bear, who heard it from his father, the old chief. Where I have differed from his account, it is because it does not correspond with those of people who were present, and who wrote about their impressions immediately afterwards, either in official reports or in private letters and papers.

Even the participants gave different versions at different times. For example, Tatum's memoirs, published in 1899, vary in some details from the reports he sent to Enoch Hoag and Jonathan Richards immediately after the incident when it was still fresh on his mind. Likewise, there is not complete agreement on what Satanta said. Some witnesses did not quote Horace Jones' translation directly, but paraphrased it. Their impressions were not always the same. This account has been drawn from Nye, above cited; from Richard Henry Pratt, *Battlefield and Classroom,* 44-46; from the Myers Papers; and Tatum's letter to Richards; and the *Army and Navy Journal,* above cited.

PART 3: THE ARREST

Josiah Butler, the agency teacher, was riding in a wagon about half way between the commissary and the school house when the shooting began. Two Kiowa warriors galloped toward him, faces painted and hair flying. Butler was sure they were going to kill him. He closed his eyes, made a quick review of his life, and commended himself to God. When he looked up again, the Indians were on either side of the wagon. Each had an arrow in his bow, pointed at Butler's heart, with a second arrow in hand.

Having made peace with the Lord, Butler began to relax and tried to strike up a conversation. The Indians did not reply. They rode alongside, arrows at ready, for the mile or so to the school. It was suppertime, and the cook was ringing the steel triangle.

"Tie up and eat supper with me," Butler told the two Indians in a mixture of Kiowa and English.

They smiled and dismounted. He motioned for them to go ahead of him, and they put their weapons away. They left after the meal, in a much better mood.[10]

Back on Grierson's porch, the most important chief who still had any influence with the military was Kicking Bird, and he was doing all he could to convince Sherman to release the others. He cited his own record as a peace chief, and promised to return the stolen mules. But the general was determined to keep Satanta, Big Tree and Satank in custody.

Kicking Bird was out of patience. Despite his own convictions, he was still a Kiowa. The honor of his people was at stake, and he was not going to stand by and let any Kiowa chief die at the end of a Texas rope.

"You have asked for those men to kill them," he told Sherman. "But they are my people, and I am not going to let you have them. You and I are going to die right here."

---

[10]Butler, "Pioneer School Teaching," 504-505.

CHAPTER 5: "YOU AND I ARE GOING TO DIE..."

For reasons of his own, Jones seems to have mistranslated the threat. Perhaps it was a mistake. More likely, he did it to prevent a general massacre there on Grierson's front porch. Whatever the reason, Sherman did not seem to understand Kicking Bird's statement, since he answered, "You and Stumbling Bear will not be killed nor harmed, as long as you continue to do well."[11]

What happened next was summed up by Lieutenant Myers:

> Lone Wolf, a Kiowa Chief, came galloping up carrying two carbines and a bow & quiver of arrows slung upon his back. Dismounting he tied his pony to the parade fence[,] laid his weapons down upon the ground while he tightened his belt and arranged his apparel and then picking up his carbine approached the porch with a smile upon his lips. Extending his arm—as if to shake hands with an officer standing next to the line of guards, while the eyes of at least thirty armed men were upon him, as some demonstration was expected, he suddenly leaped past the guards into the middle of the porch and in an instant his carbine was cocked and at the breasts of Generals Sherman and Grierson. Those standing nearby had been upon the alert though, and almost simultaneous with the click of the Indians' carbines sounded that of the thirty or forty weapons in the hands [of the] guards and citizens. The unarmed Indians seeing the futileness of the effort by Lone Wolf cried out, and laying hands on the armed warriors compelled them to desist from their desperate intentions.[12]

Although Lone Wolf was neutralized, his action started a minor brawl. Stumbling Bear had taken the bow and arrows from Lone Wolf, and was about to loose an arrow into Sherman's chest. Fearing a massacre, an Indian grabbed his arm and the arrow went wild. Grierson tackled Lone Wolf, together they fell into Kicking Bird, and all three landed in a sprawling heap.[13] Explaining what had happened, Myers wrote:

---

[11]Nye, *Carbine and Lance,* 139.
[12]Myers, Papers.
[13]Nye, *Carbine and Lance,* 141-42.

Lone Wolf was not actuated in this affair by a spirit of mere bravado or recklessness. His intention was to cover the persons of the officers mentioned with the carbines in the Indian's hands and then give them the alternative of dismissing the soldiers, and permitting the captives to depart, or dying; and the project was only frustrated by the prompt action of the guards together with the unlooked for interference of some of the unarmed Indians.[14]

Perhaps as one warrior to another, Sherman understood the situation, for he remained calm and motioned for the soldiers to lower their weapons. Lone Wolf, Stumbling Bear and Kicking Bird were allowed to get up and assured they would not be harmed. It was growing dark, now, and Sherman was anxious to end the proceedings. He demanded forty-one mules for return to Texas as reparations to Henry Warren. Lone Wolf and Kicking Bird agreed, and told the Kiowas to raise them by public subscription within the tribe. With that, the Indians fled as quickly as they could. When the chiefs returned home, they found the camps had been broken and the people had scattered into the mountains. They followed in an effort to round them up and bring them back.[15]

Eagle Heart was still on the loose, but Sherman had Satanta and Satank, whom he really wanted, along with Big Tree. They were placed in handcuffs and leg irons, in close confinement under armed guards.

"The whole garrison was wild with excitement during the day," an anonymous correspondent wrote to the *Army and Navy Journal,* "and General Sherman was extolled to the skies for his prompt and decisive action in the matter. He gave orders that the prisoners should be kept until Colonel Mackenzie of the Fourth Cavalry should come and take them down to the borders of Texas, the field of their many bloody outrages, and turn them over to the civil authorities, there to

[14]Myers, Papers.
[15]Nye, *Carbine and Lance,* 142.

be dealt with by the people as their oft-repeated crimes demand."[16]

Sherman's plans were definite. In his report to Washington, he wrote:

> These three Indians should never go forth again. If the Indian Department object to their being surrendered to a Texas jury, we had better try them by a Military Tribunal, for if from any reason in the world they go back to their tribes free, no life will be safe from Kansas to the Rio Grande. Texas has Sheriff's Courts and all the machinery of a criminal code, and I believe it will have the best effect to follow the strictly legal course, which the Indians dread far more than the shorter verdict of a rifle ball.
>
> They will confess in open court as they have already before me and twenty others that they were present aiding in a particular murder of which also there are in Jack County plenty of witnesses.

Sherman also praised Tatum for his cooperation in the affair.[17] Tatum, however, had mixed feelings. Setting down his thoughts to Sherman and Grierson, the agent wrote:

> That they are guilty of murder in the first degree, I have not the shadow of a doubt, and approve of sending Satanta, Satank and Big Tree, who are now under arrest, to Texas where the atrocity was committed, and not to be allowed to regain their freedom. But permit me to urge, and independent of my conscientiousness against capital punishment, as a matter of policy it would be best for the inhabitants of Texas, that they be not executed for some time and probably not at all; for the reason that if they are kept as prisoners, the Indians will hope to have them released and thus of a restraining influence on their actions. But if they are executed, the Kiowas will be very likely to seek revenge in the wholesale murder of white people.
>
> Please convey my views and wishes as above expressed to the proper officers in Texas in whose charge the Indian prisoners are placed.

Below Tatum's signature, there was a note which said:

[16]*Army and Navy Journal,* July 1, 1871, 735.
[17]Sherman to Townsend, May 28, 1871, Letters Received.

PART 3:   THE ARREST

Endorsement
Hdqs. of the Army
Fort Sill, May 29, 1871

Respectfully furnished Genl. Grierson, who will deliver the
within named prisoners to any officer who may be sent from Texas
to receive them, with a copy of this paper & endorsement, that due
respect may be paid to the request of the Indian Agent, till the orders
of the President may be received.

W.T. Sherman
General[18]

The endorsement was simply a procedure for all military
paperwork. The fact that Sherman respected Tatum's opinion
did not mean he agreed with it. The same day, he wrote Lieutenant General Philip H. Sheridan, whose Military Division
of the Missouri had jurisdiction over the entire central two-
thirds of the United States, "Kicking Bird and Lone Wolf
begged hard for Satanta, but I think it is time to end his
career. The Kioways [sic] accuse him of acting the woman
when you hold him prisoner, and he has been raiding in Texas
to regain his influence as a great warrior. Old Satank ought to
have been shot long ago, and Big Tree is a young warrior, the
successor of Faint Heart, who died last winter."

Referring to Sheridan's 1868-69 winter campaign, in which
the Cheyenne Chief Black Kettle and Arapaho Chief Little
Raven were killed, and Satanta and Lone Wolf had been
arrested, Sherman said, "The impudence of Satanta in coming
here to boast of his deed in Texas will satisfy you that the
Kioways need pretty much the lesson you gave Black Kettle
and Little Raven....

"Kicking Bird is about the only Kiowa that seems to understand their situation, but Lone Wolf ought to have been hung
when you had him in hand."[19]

---

[18]Tatum to Sherman and Grierson, May 29, 1871, with endorsement, Letters Received.
[19]Sherman to Sheridan, May 29, 1871, Letters Received. Sherman generally spelled the
tribe "Kioway," but was not consistent about it.

For the moment, the Kiowas were scattered and beaten. But no Kiowa chief was indispensable. It was only a matter of time before new war chiefs rose to replace those in confinement. Ultimately, events would prove Sherman right. Despite his usual sagacity, Lawrie Tatum had sadly underestimated his Indian charges.

CHAPTER 6

"We Koiet-senko Must Die"

The rain that began on the day of the massacre continued through May and into June. Sherman left for Fort Gibson on May 30, barely managing to cross Cache Creek before it became impassable. Not long afterwards, a group of Comanches came into Fort Sill from Otter Creek and reported soldiers near the mouth of the North Fork of the Red River. These were Mackenzie's troops, who had been held up by rain, mud and swollen streams. The Comanches were moving their camps to the north of the mountains by Rainy Mountain Creek. En route, they met Kicking Bird, Lone Wolf and several other Kiowa chiefs, who were trying to round up their people. They told the Comanches they "did not care what became of Satanta and Satank." The raid had made trouble for the entire tribe. Kicking Bird's faction was disgusted with the two chiefs, and after Sherman's demonstration of federal power at Fort Sill, even the war faction was in no mood for trouble over them. These developments were all reported to Colonel Grierson, who passed them on to departmental headquarters at Fort Leavenworth.[1]

Kicking Bird had reason to be unhappy. At Sherman's direction, government pressure was mounting. Before his departure, the general-in-chief had left a letter for Mackenzie,

---

[1]Grierson to AAG, Department of the Missouri, June 1, 1871, Letters Received.

saying, "Satanta, Satank and Big Tree, three of the principal Kiowas, are now here prisoners in double irons and strongly guarded, ready to be delivered to you or to a Sufficient Guard that you may send for them, to be held by the military till tried and executed by the regular process in the Criminal Courts of the locality where they committed the murder in question...."

As for the Kiowas as a whole, he said:

> They are now doubtless at their camps, on the Wichita, debating peace or war, and you should take all due precautions, as soon as you have a guard to take care of your property at Richardson.
>
> All the Calvary in Texas should operate toward the Red River and Fort Sill; communications should also be opened with this place via the Ferry at Red River Station—so that you act in concert. If parties of Indians attack soldiers or citizens, they should be followed into this Reservation till they realize that if they persist in crossing Red River they will be followed back. I think, however, that the Kiowas and Comanches of the Reservation in the arrest of Satanta, Satank, and Big Tree, will realize this and if my orders for their trial and execution in Jack County be not revised or stayed by orders from Washington [,] that property on your frontier will henceforth be more secure. Satanta says many of the mules of the train were killed and wounded; that in the attack he lost three of his warriors killed and three badly wounded, and that the warrior here killed [in the shooting during the arrest] makes seven, so he says *we are now even,* and he ought to be let off—*but I don't see it.*"[2]

On June 4, Mackenzie arrived with six companies of the Fourth Cavalry after a grueling, fruitless ride through rain and mud. He had been out of communication since the night following the massacre and was surprised to learn that his quarry was safely in irons at Fort Sill. He rested his exhausted men until June 8, when he planned to leave. Before departing, however, he met with Tatum, who was very blunt about the situation. According to Mackenzie, the agent was "anxious that the Kiowas and Comanches now out of his control be

---

[2]Sherman to Mackenzie, undated, quoted in Carter, *On the Border,* 88-89.

brought under it. This can be accomplished only by the Army. The matter is now within a very small compass. Either these Indians must be punished, or they must be allowed to murder, and rob at their own discretion."

Tatum was so adamant about taking some sort of action against the Kiowas that Mackenzie seriously considered hunting them down and bringing them in. However, it was decided that his first priority was to transport the prisoners to Texas. Then he would wait at Fort Richardson and see what the Indians did about returning Warren's mules, using the time to get his troops ready in case it was necessary to go after them.[3]

About 8 a.m., June 8, two wagons drove up to the building in which the chiefs were held. The sheets were thrown back to catch the breeze, and they had a partial load of shelled corn in their beds. At the agency school, Josiah Butler was getting ready for class when George Washington, a Caddo chief, arrived with word that all Indians were to turn out and watch the prisoners leave. He dismissed the children, and all but four went with George Washington to Fort Sill.[4]

Satanta, Satank and Big Tree were brought out, hobbling in their leg irons and blinking in the bright light. Up until then, the Indians did not believe that Sherman's orders would be carried out—that they were, in fact, going to Texas. The sight of the wagons removed any doubt. When they realized what was happening, they asked to be taken "to some post on the Arkansas." They were told it was impossible. Satanta, who apparently was still confused about the relationship between Texas and the United States, remarked "he had heard of `Washington to the East, North, and West, but never to the south'."[5]

---

[3]Mackenzie to Sherman, June 15, 1871, in Sherman, Unofficial Correspondence.

[4]Butler, "Pioneer School Teaching," 505. Although there were few, if any, Kiowas or Comanches at the agency school, the Caddoes sent their children there.

[5]Grierson to AAG, Department of the Missouri, July 9, 1871, Letters Received.

The news of their actual destination had a profound impact on the prisoners, which Butler found varied from generation to generation. "Big Tree (twenty-two years old) is anxious to live," he wrote. "Satanta (fifty years old) is indifferent as to life and Satank (seventy years old) is determined to die in preference to going to Texas."[6]

Satanta's indifference did not go as far as a hangman's rope. Momentarily losing his nerve, he put his hands on Colonel Grierson's shoulders and wailed, "My friend! My friend! My friend!" in broken English.

Satank started over to Grierson as if to shake hands. Big Tree grabbed his hands and pulled him back. Actually the old man had a knife concealed under his blanket and meant to murder the colonel. That would provoke the soldiers to start shooting and he would die a warrior's death. But Big Tree held his hands fast until they reached the lead wagon. There Satank refused to budge. Some soldiers grasped him by the hands and feet and heaved him bodily up onto the corn. Satanta and Big Tree allowed themselves to be assisted into the second wagon.

A Corporal Robinson and Private Cannon were placed in the lead wagon to guard Satank, while Private Beals and Corporal John Charlton guarded the other two. Robinson and Cannon sat on either side of Satank, backs to the sideboards. Charlton sat near the back of his wagon, with Big Tree on the left and a little to the front. Satanta faced them, with Beals on his right. All four soldiers had loaded carbines between their legs. The wagons started moving. Cavalry followed and Tonkawa Scouts from Fort Griffin rode alongside. The column was momentarily under Lieutenant William A. Thomp-

---

[6]Butler, "Pioneer School Teaching," 505-06. Butler's ages for the three chiefs were estimates. Modern research places Big Tree at about nineteen or twenty, Satanta between fifty-three and fifty-five, and Satank in his mid-seventies.

son, Fourth Cavalry, because Mackenzie had gone back to Grierson's office to go over some final details before catching up.[7]

Meanwhile, the Koiet-senko Satank had thrown his blanket over his head and covered himself completely. He began wailing and then chanted:

> *Iha hyo oya iya o ika yaya yoyo*
> *Aheyo aheyo uaheyo ya eya heyo e heyo*
> *Koiet-senko ana obahema haa ipai degi o ba ika*
> *Koiet-senko ana oba hemo hadamagagi o ba ika.*
> O sun you remain forever, but we Koiet-senko must die.
> O earth you remain forever, but we Koiet-senko must die.[8]

Horace Jones rode up to Charlton and said, "Corporal, you had better watch that Indian in the front wagon, for he intends to give you trouble."

Charlton asked why.

"Because he is chanting his death song, now," Jones explained.

He repeated the warning to Lieutenant Thompson, who replied, "We will take care of him."

As he sang, Satank was using his knife to strip the flesh from his hands and wrists so he could slip off the handcuffs. Covered by his blanket, enduring the pain and singing his death song, none of the soldiers knew what he was doing.

As the wagons reached the bottom of a hill near Cache Creek, about three quarters of a mile from the post and three hundred yards from the agency, Satank peered out and motioned to George Washington, who was riding alongside the wagon.

---

[7]Pratt, *Battlefield and Classroom,* 47; Carter. *On the Border,* 90, and *Old Sergeant,* 78; Nye, *Carbine and Lance,* 143-144; Mackenzie to Sherman, June 15, 1871, Sherman, Unofficial Correspondence.

[8]Quoted in Nye, *Carbine and Lance,* 144.

"Take this message to my people," he told George Washington in Comanche. "Tell them I died beside the road. My bones will be found there. Tell my people to gather them up and carry them away."

Then he went back under his blanket and began his death song again. Since messages were being allowed, Satanta called George Washington over and told him, "Tell the Kiowas to bring back the mules, and don't raid any more. Do as the agent tells them."

George Washington rode back up alongside the lead wagon. The second wagon followed tightly behind, the noses of its mules so close that a horseman could not pass between them. Each wagon had six mules, with the driver riding the animal nearest the wheel. The guards had begun to relax and were trying to copy Satank's song, having no idea what it meant.

Once again, Satank motioned to George Washington.

"See that tree?" he said, indicating a pecan tree a few yards ahead. "When I reach that tree, I will be dead." Then he told one of the Tonkawas, "You may have my scalp. The hair is poor. It isn't worth much, but you may have it."

The Tonkawa's wife began whooping in honor of the old Kiowa. George Washington and the scouts got out of the way. Satanta and Big Tree sat pale and rigid. The soldiers went on mimicking Satank's chant. Jones' advice had been ignored. They noticed nothing unusual. Then the chanting stopped. Satank stared up at the sky and meditated for a moment.

Suddenly he jumped up, threw the blanket completely off, and slashed at Robinson, cutting him in the leg. Robinson somersaulted backwards out of the wagon, leaving his carbine behind. Cannon jumped out as quickly as he could move. Satank grabbed Robinson's carbine and pulled down on the lever. The weapon, a seven-shot Spencer, already had a shell in the chamber, and the second shell jammed. In the rear wagon, Charlton sprang up, aimed and fired. The bullet hit Satank squarely in the chest and he went spinning around.

Big Tree put his hand on Charlton's arm and said, "No bueno!" [i.e., "Don't!"], but the corporal levered another shell into the chamber and prepared to fire again.

Thinking the Koiet-senko was dead, Lieutenant George K. Thurston, the officer of the day, gave the order to cease firing. But Satank was not dead. He sat up again on the bed of the wagon and once more began struggling to clear the carbine. Charlton fired again, and Thurston got off some rounds with his pistol. Satank was finished now. An examination of the body showed bullet wounds to the lungs, head and right wrist, as well as other parts of his body. The teamster driving the wagon was badly wounded. He had remained on his mule when the shooting started, and Charlton had not seen him behind the loose sheets. The corporal always believed one of his bullets went completely through Satank and struck the teamster.

In the second wagon, Satanta and Big Tree sat with raised hands. Trumpeter Oxford rode up.

"Who killed Satank?" he asked.

"I did, but I am afraid I'll catch hell for doing it," Charlton replied.

A few minutes later, Mackenzie arrived and asked the same question.

"Corporal Charlton," Oxford said.

Mackenzie told Charlton to search Satanta and Big Tree thoroughly. When that was done, he ordered the column to begin moving again. Big Tree looked back and saw Satank's body lying in the dust with blood flowing from his mouth. As Caddo George Washington turned back toward Fort Sill, Satanta called out to him, "Tell the Kiowas that I may never see any of them again, but I now wish them to be at peace with the whites."

The Tonkawas "begged hard" for the scalp, since Satank had killed several of their people. When the soldiers wouldn't let them take it, they begged for his bloodstained blanket instead. That request was granted. In keeping with Satank's last request, the Kiowas were offered the body. They refused to come in for it, and a burial detail interred him in the post cemetery at Fort Sill.[9]

After the death of Satank, Mackenzie was taking no chances with his prisoners. They were watched constantly, the entire 123 miles from Fort Sill to Fort Richardson. Fearing the Kiowas were shadowing the column and would attempt to free them, he had pickets and outposts thrown up well out from the camp each night. Herd guards were strengthened to prevent any attackers from stampeding the horses. The two prisoners were bedded down by stretching them length-wise out on the ground, their hands lashed to a stake above their heads and their feet lashed to a second stake. Guards were placed over them.

In the swamps of the Wichita, the entire camp was attacked by large mosquitoes. The soldiers built fires out of green logs and slept in the smoke to keep them away. They wore their gauntlets to bed and fabricated mosquito nets to little avail. The Indians had no such protection, and their cries and grunts could be heard all night.[10]

It was too much for Charlton. Regardless of how he per-

---

[9]Pratt, *Battlefield and Classroom*, 47; Carter, *Old Sergeant*, 78-79, and *On the Border*, 91, 96; Nye, *Carbine and Lance*, 145-47. Nye quoted Lieutenant Thurston's report on 45-46, citing RG 94 1305 AGO 1871, i.e. Letters Received, as his source. However, the report was not in the file as of January 1988 when a microfilm copy was obtained. Carter said the Tonkawas took the scalp. But Butler ("Pioneer School Teaching," 507) and Nye said the soldiers refused. I have opted for the latter version, since Butler was close to the scene and wrote his account almost immediately afterwards, while Carter heard it second hand.

[10]Carter, *On the Border*, 95-96.

sonally felt about the two Kiowas, Mackenzie's procedures seemed unduly harsh. One night just before dark, he went over to where they were staked out, and watched as Satanta's muscles swelled and strained at the ropes. The Kiowa was covered with mosquitoes and the sweat rolled down from his body as they bit into him.

"Old fellow," Charlton said, "war is hell and you're a blood thirsty savage, but by criminy, I'm not and I'll be damned if those mosquitoes shall bite you while you are helpless."

He told the sentinels to fan both prisoners with branches to keep the mosquitoes off. They did this every night until they reached Jacksboro.[11]

According to Lieutenant Carter, whose memoirs were written with a flair for the dramatic, the column was met by crowds of people and the regimental band when it rode into Fort Richardson on June 15. But Jehu Atkinson, who recalled the event in 1947 when he was probably the last person alive who remembered it, said Mackenzie entered the post without fanfare, and had the prisoners safely in the guardhouse before local citizens even realized the column had returned.[12]

The big problem now was security. Several of the murdered teamsters had lived in Jacksboro. Feeling against the chiefs ran high and there had been threats against them. The guardhouse was just across a creek from a dense chaparral, and it would have been easy for a sniper to pick off the two Indians as they were being led in or out of the building. Austin *State Journal* correspondent E.F. Gilbert wrote, "You can scarcely stop at a house, but some member of the family has lost a friend or relative to the quivering arrow of the lurking savage. Is it any wonder, then, that a bitter feeling should be engendered against the whole race of savages?" So a strong guard

---

[11]Charlton to Carter, January 12, 1921, in Carter, *Old Sergeant*, 81.
[12]Carter, *On the Border*, 97-98; Huckabay, *Ninety-four Years*, 178.

was placed around the building. This trial was the ultimate test of white man's justice. Above all else, the army intended to avoid a lynching.[13]

The army wasn't the only organization interested in protecting the prisoners. In the east, the Quakers were beginning to react, particularly since one of their own had been involved in the arrest. One influential Friend, John Garrett of Philadelphia, wrote Tatum "partly to express my sympathy with thee in thy responsible service for the Master—but more especially at this time to encourage to use every proper effort to secure for Satanta & his companions in crime a punishment consistent with the precepts of Christianity. I rejoice that there is a prospect of their trial by civil process, & that these unruly Kiowas are likely to learn that wrong-doing on their part will bring upon them the same penalties as like conduct would bring upon the pale faces.

"But how earnestly do I desire that their lives may be spared, & Christian influences brought to bear for their conversion & salvation.

"Will not the effect upon the tribe be far better for these criminals to be held in close confinement during their natural lives than for them to receive the common penalty for murder in the first degree?" Garrett asked. For his own part, he said, "I am apprehensive that the feeling of the white frontiersman is such that they will demand immediate trial, conviction and execution."[14]

Garrett apparently failed to consider that as he sat safely in Philadelphia, these "white frontiersmen" were being burned, looted, kidnapped and murdered. And while the soldiers and Quakers feared angry citizens, the citizens feared the Indians. Nobody in Jacksboro knew what was going on in the Indian

---

[13]Carter, *On the Border*, 98; Gilbert, Austin *State Journal*, July 11, 1871.

[14]John B. Garrett to Tatum, June 14, 1871, Kiowa File.

Territory, or where the Kiowas might be. Large Indian trails were reported in the immediate vicinity, and people feared that if the chiefs were executed, the town might be attacked "some night when least expected." Since Fort Richardson was half a mile away, and on the other side of the creek, "much damage and bloodshed might be effected before assistance could be obtained."[15]

The legal system had similar fears. Jack County was part of the 13th Judicial District headquartered in Parker County. Trials were held in Jacksboro on a circuit basis with the court and attorneys coming from Weatherford. Jack County itself was large in relation to the transportation of that time, and travel to court involved long, lonely stretches of open country. The Warren Wagon Train Massacre had terrorized the entire frontier and the attorneys felt the risk was too great. Accordingly, they petitioned District Judge Charles Soward not to hold court in Jacksboro, saying, "that it is well known and indisputable fact that the County of Jack and the whole country between this place and Jacksborough [*sic*] is to an unusual and very dangerous extent infested with large bands of hostile Indians, and that on this account travel between this [place] and Jacksborough is unusually dangerous...."[16]

Judge Soward denied the motion. A grand jury was impaneled, and on July 4, 1871, it found that:

> Satanta and Big Tree, late of the County and State aforesaid, with force and malice not having the fear of God before their eyes, but being moved and seduced by the instigation of the devil...the said S. Long, James Elliott, N.J. Baxter, James Williams, Samuel Elliott, John Mullins and James Bowman wilfully, unlawfully, feloniously and by their malice aforethought did kill and murder contrary to the form of the statute on such case made and provided, and against the peace and dignity of the State of Texas.

---

[15]Gilbert, Austin *State Journal*, July 11, 1871.
[16]Quoted in Huckabay, *Ninety-Four Years*, 181.

PART 3: THE ARREST

The indictment was signed by S.W. Eastin, foreman, and Samuel W.T. Lanham, district attorney.[17] A native of Spartanburg, South Carolina, Lanham had served in the Confederate Army and came to Texas after the war. Now, on his twenty-fifth birthday, he was about to prosecute one of the most important cases in Texas history.

As the State of Texas prepared to go to trial, the waves were being felt across the nation. It began with Henry Warren, the man who owned the ruined wagon train. Like most businessmen he operated on borrowed capital, and with the supplies for Fort Griffin destroyed, it was unlikely the government would pay his drafts. If that was the case, he would go into default and that, in turn, would seriously damage the Fort Worth banking firm of Couts and Fain, which held his notes. But the bank had influential friends who traveled to Washington to present the case to the government. While it was being decided, news arrived that the chiefs had been arrested and the mules returned. The drafts were paid.

The announcement about the mules was premature. Although Grierson was optimistic, and reported that Kicking Bird had already obtained eleven and would probably deliver the balance, the chief was having trouble. The Kiowas were starting to recover from the shock of the arrest. Mules in hand were worth more than Indians in prison. They were beginning to balk at the idea of returning the animals, and Kicking Bird was almost ready to give up.[18]

In Washington, relations between the military and the Indian Bureau were being reevaluated. A Department of the Interior circular in 1869 had put such restrictions on the army in reservations that troops were loathe to enter the areas at all.

---

[17] Ibid., 180-81.

[18] Ibid., 173; Grierson to AAG, Department of the Missouri, July 9, 1871, Letters Received; Nye, *Carbine and Lance*, 143.

Prosecutor
Samuel W. T.
Lanham in later
life. *Texas State
Library and
Archive.*

Events at Jacksboro and Fort Sill made it obvious that the
military must have some authority to act on the reservations
or there would be chaos.

Accordingly, Interior Secretary Columbus Delano told
Indian Commissioner Ely S. Parker to "inform the War
Department that hereafter and until otherwise advised by
your office, the military authorities may be permitted to enter
the Indian Territory at all times in the pursuit and arrest of the
predatyr [*sic*] and criminal Indians and for the purpose of
recovering property and captives held by such Indians. I

would also suggest that when the military thus enter the Indian territory they take with them an Indian Agent or Superintendent, if practicable, not to command the expedition but to witness the proceedings." The following day, Parker notified the War Department of the change.[19]

Meanwhile, the whole nation was watching events in a town of some three hundred people on the rolling prairie at the edge of west Texas.

[19]Parker to W.W. Belknap, Secretary of the War, June 21, 1871; Delano to Parker, June 20, 1871, both in Letters Received. Parker himself was a Seneca Indian.

Part 4: The Trial

CHAPTER 7

"Satanta Ought to Have Been Hung and That Would Have Ended the Trouble"

On Wednesday, July 5, 1871, trial began in Cause No. 224, the State of Texas vs. Satanta and Big Tree. Carter and Lanham had already discussed security arrangements. Twenty soldiers formed a screen around the guardhouse as the prisoners were led out. That way, no one could shoot at them from the surrounding brush without hitting one of the guards. From there, they accompanied the Indians over the quarter-mile trail through the brush from Fort Richardson to the new, two-story courthouse. Jacksboro was packed with spectators and news correspondents. Classes at the local school, in session despite the summer, were dismissed for the occasion. This was more than the trial of two Kiowas—the entire federal Indian policy was on trial, and the Quakers knew it.

"The eyes of many in various parts of the country are turned toward the Kiowa Agency," Friend William Nicholson wrote Tatum from the Central Superintendency in Lawrence. "Some are hoping every day to hear of increased trouble & difficulty in that quarter that they may have a just ground for denouncing the President's pacific policy as a failure—whilst the friends of that policy are equally hoping and hopeful to hear more favorable news."[1]

---

[1]Nicholson to Tatum, August 22, 1871, Kiowa File.

In the small, second floor courtroom, Lanham shuffled his papers. Satanta and Big Tree came in, wrapped in blankets with the manacles clanking as they walked. They were accompanied by their attorneys and Horace Jones, the Fort Sill interpreter. Spectators swarmed in after them until the thirty-by-thirty-foot room could hold no more.[2]

Defense attorneys Thomas Ball and J.A. Woolfork opened the proceedings by challenging the state's right to try the defendants, since they contended the Indians were wards of the federal government. Lanham took exception and was upheld by the court. The state then announced it was ready to go to trial. With that, the defense attorneys asked that Big Tree's trial be severed from Satanta's. Soward granted the request and Big Tree entered a plea of not guilty. Fifty jurors were called out, from which twelve were empaneled and seated on two long wooden benches.[3]

In his popular memoirs of the trial, Carter called the panel the "cowboy jury" and portrayed its members as gun-toting rustics, an image which has been carried down to modern times. Although juror Peter Lynn was a cattleman, other members of the panel, such as Daniel Brown, Evert Johnson Jr. and Stanley Cooper, were respected merchants. The remaining jurors were John Cameron, H.B. Verner, William Hensley, John H. Brown, Peter Hart, L.P. Bunch, James Cooley, and Thomas W. Williams, foreman. Most, if not all, were among the area's leading citizens.[4]

Ball opened the case for the defense with a plea for compassion. Referring to Indians in general as "my brother," he catalogued their sufferings at the hands of the whites, of how

---

[2]Carter, *On the Border*, 99-101; Wilbarger, *Indian Depredations*, 561; Huckabay, *Ninety-four Years*, 138. The description of the courthouse is from Mrs. Huckabay.

[3]Jack Country, District Court Minutes, A:235; Wilbarger, *Indian Indepredations*, 562.

[4]McConnell, *Five Years a Cavalryman*, 282; Carter, "The Cowboys' Verdict," 301-05. Biographical sketches of several of the jurors can be found in Huckabay, *Ninety-four Years*, 453 ff.

they had been repeatedly cheated of their lands and driven westward until it seemed like they had no where else to go. Any depredations were simply the instinctive retaliation of any creature which had been pushed to the limit of endurance.

The day grew hot, and Ball grew more eloquent as he took off his coat and recounted historic abuses of Indians beginning with the Spanish Conquest. He described Cortez and Montezuma, and how the Spaniards had roasted the last Aztec Emperor Cuauhtemoc on a bed of coals. Finally, he invoked the eagle as the symbol of American freedom and urged the jury to allow the two Kiowas to "fly away as free and unhampered." When that particular reference was interpreted to Satanta and Big Tree, they grunted and nodded approval. Until this point, they had been expecting to be summarily put to death, and hardly understood the proceedings. Now it seemed to them they had a slim chance for release.[5]

The state's primary witnesses were Jones, Mackenzie, and Brazeal, the wounded teamster. The orderly sergeant, Miles Varily, also testified. Lawrie Tatum was represented by Mathew Leeper, the agency interpreter. Leeper was important because he had actually understood Satanta's boasting, while Tatum only got it in translation. The agent himself did not attend. The witnesses were questioned closely about the affair. The trial went rapidly after that, and soon it was time for the closing arguments.[6]

The prosecution went first. The people of Texas were now on center stage and the power over the two Kiowas rested in their hands. Lanham used the chance to sum up all their fears

---

[5]Carter, *On the Border*, 100-01. Ball's reference to Cuauhtemoc (spelled "Gautemozin" in Carter and other old texts) is erroneous. He was not placed on a bed of coals; his feet were burned during interrogation. He survived the torture as the Spaniards intended he would. Ball obviously was trying to excuse the Kiowas' roasting of Elliot by inferring there were white precedents for that kind of death, even if they had supposedly occurred 350 years earlier.

[6]Ibid., 101; Tatum, *Red Brothers,*, 121-22.

and frustrations, and their disgust at those who supported their enemies and profited from their sufferings.

> This is a novel and important trial, and has, perhaps, no precedent in the history of American criminal jurisprudence [he began]. The remarkable character of the prisoners, who are leading representatives of their race; their crude and barbarous appearance; the gravity of the charge; the number of victims; the horrid brutality and inhuman butchery inflicted upon the bodies of the dead; the dreadful and terrific spectacle of seven men, who were husbands, fathers, brothers, sons and lovers, on the morning of the dark and bloody day of this atrocious deed, and rose from their rude tents bright with hope, in the prime and pride of manhood—found, at a later hour, beyond recognition in every condition of horrid disfiguration, unutterable mutilation and death...."

Safe from the depredations on the plains, the Indian appeasers of the east had been duped by stories of Logan and Pocahontas, Lanham said. They saw Satanta as "the veteran council chief of the Kiowas—the orator, the diplomat, the counselor of his tribe—the pulse of his race", while Big Tree was "the mighty warrior athlete, with the speed of the deer and the eye of the eagle...."

But the people of Texas, who lived in daily dread of Indian raids, saw them differently.

> We recognize in Satanta the arch fiend of treachery and blood—the cunning Cataline—the promoter of strife—the breaker of treaties signed by his own hand—the inciter of his fellows to rapine and murder—the artful dealer in bravado while in the pow-wow, and the most abject coward in the field, as well as the most canting and double-tongued hypocrite when detected and overcome! In Big Tree we perceive the tiger-demon, who has tasted blood and loves it as his food—who stops at no crime, how black soever—who is swift at every species of ferocity, and pities not at any sight of agony or death—he can scalp, burn, torture, mangle and deface his victims with all the superlatives of cruelty, and have no feeling of sympathy or remorse. They are both hideous and loathsome in appearance, and

we look in vain to see in them anything to be admired, or even endured.

Despite the sufferings on the plains, Lanham told the jury every effort had been made to rouse public sympathy for the tribes, to provide them with annuities and protection. At the same time, the Indian problem had been used to profit corrupt politicians at the expense of the settlers. Because of this, the tribes had

> kindled the flames around the cabin of the pioneer and despoiled him of his hard earnings, murdered and scalped our people, and carried off our women into captivity worse than death. For many years, predatory and numerous bands of these "pets of the government" have waged the most relentless and heartrending warfare upon our frontier, stealing our property and killing our citizens. We have cried aloud for help; as segments of the grand aggregate of the country we have begged for relief; deaf ears have been turned to our cries, and the story of our wrongs has been discredited.

The only reason the chiefs had even been brought to trial for the Warren massacre, and the only reason stolen property was now being returned, was that Sherman himself had been present when it occurred

> for it is a fact, well known in Texas, that stolen property has been traced to the very doors of the reservation, and there identified by our people, to no purpose. We are greatly indebted to the military arm of the government for kindly offices and co-operation in procuring the arrest and transference of the defendants. If the entire management of the Indian question were submitted to that gallant and distinguished officer, General Mackenzie, who graces this occasion with his dignified presence, our frontier would soon enjoy the immunity from these marauders.

Lanham reminded the jury that despite their own methods of dealing death, the Indians were entitled to all the same rights of trial, according to the same rules and procedures as any other person. With this in mind, he reviewed the evidence.

The defendants had been absent from the reservation at Fort Sill during the time in question.

They had enough time to ride into Texas, commit the raid and return.

Upon their return, they brought forty mules along with firearms and supplies belonging to the victims.

Satanta himself had admitted to the interpreter, to Tatum and to Sherman that he, along with Big Tree and Satank, had committed the raid. Neither of the latter two had refuted him.

The description of the Warren raid given by one of the survivors matched Satanta's description.

A member of the burial detail had described the scene and identified Kiowa weapons.

> The same amount and character of testimony were sufficient to convict any white man. "By their own words let them be condemned." Their conviction and punishment can not repair the loss, nor avenge the blood of the good men they have slain; still, it is due to law, justice and humanity that they should receive the highest punishment. This is even too mild and humane for them. Pillage and bloodthirstiness were the motors of this diabolical deed—fondness for torture and intoxication of delight at human agony impelled its perpetration. All the elements of murder in the first degree are found in the case. The jurisdiction of the court is complete, and the State of Texas expects from you a verdict and judgment in accordance with the law and evidence.[7]

[7]All that remains of the official record are the minutes of the trial contained in the docket book, military files, and the C.C. Rister Papers at Texas Tech University. The complete record had already disappeared by 1877, when historical inquiries were first made. Thus, with the cases of Satanta and Big Tree severed, we cannot be certain in which trial Lanham made his speech, nor Satanta his rebuttal. The sequence of speeches, i.e.Ball, Lanham, Woolfork, and Satanta, is a matter of general agreement in all accounts. I have placed Lanham's remarks at the close of Big Tree's trial, which was the first, since Lanham mentioned Big Tree and called for a guilty verdict. I have placed Satanta's reply in his own trial, because he was speaking for himself, rather than Big Tree. Lanham's speech has been printed in many memoirs and histories, both in the nineteenth century and in the first half of the twentieth. This version is from Wilbarger, *Indian Depredations*, 562-66. Carter's somewhat fanciful description of the jury appeared in an article in *Youth's Companion* (reprinted in McConnell, *Five Years a Cavalryman*, 305) and fifty years later in *On the Border*, 101.

Now it was the defense's turn. Where Ball had sought compassion in his opening statements, Woolfork closed by trying to awe or intimidate. He took off his coat, vest, collar and tie, rolled up his shirtsleeves and spoke directly to Williams, the foreman of the jury. He shook his finger at him and gestured "in the most emphatic, even violent manner." Williams was unimpressed. The judge charged the jurors, who retired and deliberated for half an hour before returning with the verdict.[8]

The formal record of verdict and sentencing states:

> We the Jury find the Defendant Big Tree, GUILTY of murder in the 1st degree and assess the punishment at *Death*.
>
> Thos. W. Williams
Foreman of the jury.

> It is therefore ordered and adjudged and decreed by the Court that the said Defendant, Big Tree be taken by the Sheriff and hanged until he (Big Tree) is dead, dead, dead! And may the Lord have mercy on his Soul! And it is further ordered that the Sheriff [is] to take the said Defendant into close custody and hold him to await the sentence of this Court upon the Judgment herein.[9]

Court adjourned for the day. Mackenzie noted with some satisfaction, "Big-tree was tried and sentenced to death to day. Satanta, if a jury can be impanelled, will be tried to morrow, and as the evidence is much stronger in his case than in Big-tree's, the result is not doubtful."[10]

The result may have been a foregone conclusion, but Satanta did not intend to sit quietly through it. When court

---

[8]Carter, *On the Border*, 101-102, and "The Cowboys' Verdict," 305-06; Austin *State Journal*, July 18, 1871.

[9]Jack County, District Court Minutes, A:236. Far from being melodramatic, the phrase "dead, dead, dead" has a practical legal purpose. There was a certain possibility that the rope might break, or too much stretch or slack might allow the condemned man to hit the ground. In such a case, he might claim freedom on the grounds that he had been legally executed and survived. A triple death sentence covered these occasions, since it gave the state a chance to haul him up and hang him again. (See Ed Coonfield, "The Fine Art of Hanging," 29).

[10]Extract from Commanding Officer, Fort Richardson (i.e., Mackenzie), AAG Department of Texas, July 13, 1871, Letters Received.

reconvened with the same jury the following morning, the old orator had plenty to say in his own behalf. He spoke in Comanche, using a combination of speech and sign, both interpreted by Jones.

"Why should I lie, since I have been under the control of the white people since boy-hood," Satanta began, and indicated the height of a child with his hand. "I started off with a party of my people for Texas, and stopped with a sick man on the Peasis [*sic*] river.

"I have been abused by my tribe for being too friendly with the white man. I have always been an advocate for peace. I have always wished this to be made a country of white people."

Holding up his arms to show the handcuffs, he continued:

I am wearing shackles because of the Kiowas and General Sherman. I am to suffer for what others did.

This is the first time I have ever faced Texans. They know me not—neither do I know them. If you let me live, I feel my ability to control my people. If I die it will be like a match put to the prairie. No power can stop it. If I could see General Grierson and my people, I pledge myself that neither I nor my people will ever cross Red River again. That river shall be the long line. I am willing to pledge myself for the Kiowas, that if you grant my freedom, I will make permanent peace with the white man—Whatever mischief has been done, has been done by the Kiowas. This is the first time I have ever entered the war-path against the white man. If released, I will pledge myself in behalf of the Kiowas for a lasting peace. I have but little knowledge of the Texas people now. I have never understood them as a people. Release me, and your people may go on undisturbed, with their farming and stock raising—all will go well.

Referring to his detention during Sheridan's winter campaign, Satanta said.

When General Sherman [*sic*] and General Caster [*sic*] had me arrested they did not put upon me the indignity of wearing these shackles. I could go about with my limbs untrammelled. I have seen these people—men, women and children in this council room for two days, and I have said in my heart, I am willing to make peace. Take off these shackles. I cannot treat now—I feel myself as a woman.

I expect to hear of mischief done by my people on this frontier. I think they are now waiting my return or anticipating my death. Gen. Grierson and my father, General [*sic*] Tatum, are now anxiously awaiting to hear from me.

Big Bow, Fast Bear, Eagle Heart and Parah [Parra-o-coom, a Comanche chief] have been committing depredations in Texas. I feel more enmity against them than I do against the Texans. I will kill them with my own hands if I am permitted to return to my home.[11]

The jury didn't buy it. Satanta likewise was convicted and sentenced to death. Ball and Woolfork immediately filed motions for a new trial for the two Kiowas. Soward heard their arguments and overruled them. The defense filed exceptions, after which Satanta and Big Tree were sentenced to die on September 1.[12]

Texas was jubilant. The Austin *State Journal* said Satanta's execution

will do more than anything else to convince these chronic and untameable robbers, that the policy of permitting open, incessant and bloody assaults on our line of settlements by these marauders, has been brought to a permanent close.—Let it henceforth be understood, far and wide, that while our Government is making every effort to protect, civilize and christianize the well disposed and peaceable Indians, those who still persist in deeds of robbery and murder will be accordingly punished for their crimes, the same as are white criminals. With the inauguration of this policy our long harassed and bleeding border will at last have peace.[13]

---

[11]This version of Satanta's speech was taken down by E.F. Gilbert in Jacksboro, and published in the Austin *State Journal* on July 18, 1871, only twelve days after the trial. It is a classic piece of Satanta's oratory as translated by Jones, who was fluent in English and Comanche. In February 1888, almost seventeen years later, Carter's version appeared in *Youth's Companion*, and was reprinted in McConnell, *Five Years a Cavalryman*, 286-87, and in Wilbarger, *Indian Depredation*, 567-68. It is an extract, rather than the complete speech, and is rendered into something resembling pidgin. It is unworthy of Satanta as an orator or Jones as an interpreter, and is now generally considered to be an "imperfect" record.

[12]Jack County, District Court Minutes, A:237-38.

[13]Austin *State Journal*, July 18, 1871.

The news of the trial and sentence was flashed across the nation. On July 16, the New York *Times* reported the convictions and said Colonel J.J. Reynolds, departmental commander, had ordered the chiefs held until instructions could be received from the president.[14] The pro-Indian lobby was already working on the federal government to obtain some sort of clemency. Three days later, Enoch Hoag wrote Grant, urging executive clemency.

The eastern and Quaker factions were not alone in their concern for the fate of the two Kiowas. There were those close to the case, but personally dispassionate, who also questioned the wisdom of the death penalty. When the court session ended, Judge Soward returned to Weatherford where, on July 10, he wrote Governor Edmund Davis:

> Mr. Tatem [*sic*] expressed a strong desire that they should be punished by imprisonment for life, instead of death, but the jury thought differently. I passed sentence upon them on the eighth of July, and fixed the time of execution at Friday, September 1, next. I must say, here, that I concur with Mr. Tatem as to the punishment; simply, however, upon a politic view of the matter. Mr. Tatem has indicated that if they are tried, convicted and punished by imprisonment, that he would render the civil authorities all the assistance in his power to bring others of those tribes on the reservation who have been guilty of outrages in Texas to trial and just punishment. I would have petitioned your excellency to commute their punishment to imprisonment for life, were it not that I know a great majority of the people on the frontier demand their execution. Your excellency, however, acting for the weal of the State at large, and free from the passions of the masses, may see fit to commute their punishment. If so, I say amen![15]

Davis agreed. On August 2, he issued a proclamation commuting their sentences to life imprisonment at hard labor, citing the opinion that it would be a calming influence on the

---

[14]New York *Times*, July 16, 1871.
[15]Soward to Davis, July 18, 1871, quoted in Wilbarger, *Indian Depredations*, 569–80.

Kiowas. However, he went one step further, questioning whether the Warren massacre could even be considered murder under the state statutes, because it was "an act of Savage Warfare."[16]

That was too much for Sherman.

"Satanta ought to have been hung and that would have ended the trouble," he fumed, "but his sentence has been commuted to life imprisonment, and I know these Kioways well enough to see that they will be everlastingly pleading for his release. He should never be released, and I hope the War Department will never consent to his return to his tribe. As to Big Tree, I do not deem his imprisonment so essential though he ought to keep Satanta company."

Sherman added that Kicking Bird could keep the Kiowas under control if Satanta were out of the way, and doubted that Kicking Bird actually wanted Satanta returned. Instead, he said Kicking Bird's petitions for Satanta's release were simply a means of maintaining prestige with his people.[17]

The citizens of Texas, and particularly on the frontier, were outraged. Here had been their chance to take decisive action in their own defense. It had been snatched away from them by state and federal governments which—in their view—had refused to defend them. The state penitentiary was in Huntsville, deep in east Texas, weeks away from Jacksboro and, given the mood of the public, Davis asked for a military escort to make certain Satanta and Big Tree got there alive. Colonel Reynolds ordered the commanding officer at Fort Richardson (Mackenzie was then in the field) to deliver the prisoners "under suitable guard" to the warden in Huntsville. The officer of the guard would be directly responsible both for the custody and personal safety of the chiefs until they were formally delivered to the warden. There was to be no commu-

---

[16]Edmund J. Davis, proclamation, August 2, 1871, copy in the C.C. Rister Papers.
[17]Quoted in Nye, *Carbine and Lance,* 147.

nication between the prisoners and any civilians en route. The officer of the guard was to get a receipt and forward it to departmental headquarters in San Antonio.[18]

Some time was required before arrangements could be completed, during which the prisoners remained in the guardhouse at Fort Richardson. In good weather, they were taken out and allowed to walk around the corrals and laundresses' quarters for fresh air and exercise. They were always under guard and their legirons and handcuffs were never removed except in one instance. That was when Satanta developed a severe case of "guardhouse itch", and his handcuffs were taken off so he could scratch his ankles and apply a salve prescribed by the post surgeon.[19] On October 16, Satanta and Big Tree left for Huntsville, guarded by a company of 11th Infantry under Captain H.L. Chapman.[20]

The Texans received some consolation. Sherman was now firmly on their side. On September 2, Secretary of War W.W. Belknap was able to write a concerned citizen in Weatherford, "Every precaution which the limited resources of the Army will allow is taken to ensure the safety of the inhabitants of the Frontier."[21]

[18]Headquarters, Department of Texas and Louisiana, Special Order No. 185, September 12, 1871, Letters Received.

[19]Carter, *On the Border,* 103.

[20]Post Returns, Fort Richardson, Texas, October 1871.

[21]Belknap to William Long, September 2, 1871, Letters Received.

CHAPTER 8

"Hang Every Murderer and Robber Among Them"

While Texas was having its day in court, the repercussions of the arrest of Satanta and Big Tree were spreading deep into the Indian Territory. The military and agency authorities on that frontier had every reason to believe the Kiowas would combine with one or more of the other plains tribes and mount a major war throughout the territory. If that happened, the best the soldiers could hope for would be to hold until additional troops were sent from Kansas.

The threat was very real. Ironically, the Comanches chose to sit on the sidelines. The Kiowas had brought this one on themselves, and their allies felt no particular obligation to help them out of it. Thus the military command in the territory found itself increasingly forced to rely on the goodwill of one of its toughest adversaries.

The problem began the day Sherman left, when the Indians attacked a ranch on the Red River east of the mouth of Cache Creek. Three hostiles and a settler were killed before they were repulsed. In itself this was an isolated incident. But given the general instability brought on by the arrests, it could have been a sign of things to come. When Grierson learned an unguarded wagon train was approaching Fort Sill with arms and ordnance, he sent a detachment to meet it and bring it in.[1]

---

[1]Grierson to AAG, Department of the Missouri, June 1, 1871, Letters Received.

On June 14, two Kiowas came to the Caddo and Co-
manche camps to hear the latest news from Fort Sill. George
Washington told them about the death of Satank and
Satanta's message for his people. The Kiowas started for home
immediately but, before they arrived, an Arapaho came to the
Kiowa camp with a rumor that Satank had been killed at Fort
Sill, and that Satanta and Big Tree had been killed en route to
Texas. Excitement swept through both the Kiowas and some
visiting Cheyennes. A war dance was held and the two groups
declared they would fight.

Still, Grierson hoped to keep the lid on. A Caddo, who had
been visiting the Kiowa camp at the time, told authorities at
the fort that they were "well disposed" until the Arapaho
arrived with the rumor. In fact, he said Kicking Bird had finally
managed to get the forty-one-mule indemnity together, and
was about to deliver the animals. The Comanches felt that
once the Kiowas learned Satanta and Big Tree were still alive,
they would settle down, particularly if they understood that
their good behavior would go far in determining the fate of the
two prisoners.

"I think that unless the Kiowas succeed in forming a *strong
combination* with the Cheyennes, and get the Comanches to
join them, that they will not go to war, even if Satanta and Big
Tree are both hanged in Texas, for the murders they have
committed," Grierson wrote.

Still, he said that if the Indians did not calm down before
the arrival of the additional companies from Camp Supply
and Fort Dodge, then he would "move out to the Kiowa
camps, with sufficient force to quiet them.

"It will be my object to do this in such a manner as to give
Kicking Bird and other Kiowas who are less inclined to be
hostile, an opportunity to separate from those who may be
more desirous for war."[2]

---

[2]Grierson to AAG, Department of the Missouri, June 19, 1871, ibid.

The prospect of trouble spreading was raised on July 10, when Brinton Darlington, agent to the Cheyennes and Arapahos, sent a two-sentence note to Lieutenant Colonel J.W. Davidson, Tenth Cavalry, commanding officer at Camp Supply.

> Having learned from various sources that the Kiowa Indians have been laboring unremittingly to draw the Cheyennes into a general Indian War.
>
> Therefore I deem it important that they should not in any considerable numbers, be permitted to come upon the Reservations north of the Washita river.[3]

About this time, a shadowy figure appeared at Camp Supply. It was the Do-ha-te Maman-ti. He was so little known outside Kiowa circles that Davidson did not realize he was dealing with the architect and true leader of the Warren massacre and other raids into Texas. In his report, he referred to Maman-ti as "a Kiowa Chief of some note (I am informed)...."

Maman-ti told Davidson that the entire Kiowa nation was camped along with a major portion of the Comanches within 125 miles of Camp Supply. With that in mind, he wanted to hold a parley.

Davidson refused to be stampeded. He asked Maman-ti if the mules had been delivered to Fort Sill according to Sherman's instructions. If not, he said they had nothing to talk about. He did, however, tell the Do-ha-te that the government henceforth intended to "hang every murderer and robber among them upon conviction by the Civil Courts, instead of killing them as soldiers in battle."

Maman-ti said he would return to his camp, and bring Davidson proof within the next five days, that the mules were on their way to Fort Sill.

Davidson did not like the Kiowa movements northward, nor their close proximity to the Cheyennes. He sent a copy of

---

[3]Darlington to Davidson, July 10, 1871, ibid.

Darlington's letter to the assistant adjutant general of the
Department of the Missouri at Fort Leavenworth, with a
cover letter outlining his misgivings. He also pointed out that
Maman-ti was the brother-in-law of the Cheyenne Chief Little Robe, "and the ties of intermarriage are abundant between
the two tribes."

"I ask another mounted company be sent me in order that I
may have sufficient force to keep these Kiowas back upon
their Reservation, or that Agent Darlington's letter be referred
to the Commander at Fort Sill that he may do it," Davidson
wrote.

"The whole Cheyenne nation are camped on Wolf [Creek]
within 14 miles of me killing buffalo for lodge skins, and it
will require some force and much watchfulness to prevent the
Kiowas from being constantly among them."[4]

There were reasons for Davidson's concern. Throughout
the previous winter some younger Cheyennes had been riding
with Kiowas and Comanches on their raids into Texas. In January, the Cheyenne Chief Big Jake told Darlington that five of
his warriors had gone to Texas, where they had killed a man
and stolen some horses. But they failed to gain support from
the rest of the tribe, which had refused to join in their victory
dance.

By and large, the Cheyennes remained friendly, or at least
neutral. Part of this was due to the efforts of both Darlington
and Davidson to maintain cordial relations with the chiefs.[5]
Another factor was that during the first part of the summer,
when the Satanta furor was at its height, Little Robe and
Stone Calf, another powerful Cheyenne chief, were touring
the east and could easily have become hostages. The chiefs
themselves were well received and had the opportunity to pre-

[4]Davidson to AAG, Department of the Missouri, July 10, 1871, ibid.
[5]Berthrong, *Southern Cheyennes*, 358-59.

sent their grievances to eastern sympathizers. They returned to their homes impressed by the white man's civilization and awed by his numbers and his power.

Back on the reservation, Darlington kept a close watch on his charges throughout the season, and cultivated the friendly chiefs. In late summer, several of the chiefs visited the agent before leaving for the buffalo ranges. They departed on such good terms that a month later, when word came that some Cheyennes had stolen livestock in Texas, Darlington presumed the animals would be returned without much trouble. He was right. Davidson was able to get them back, and by November 3 had delivered them to the agency.[6]

The war faction of the Kiowas was becoming increasingly isolated as its support dwindled. The arrest of Satanta, Satank and Big Tree had been a demonstration of raw federal power along with the determination to use it. And Judge Soward had made it clear to Tatum that in exchange for intercession on behalf of the Kiowas convicted in his court, he expected the return of stolen Texas property.[7] With these factors, Kicking Bird's prestige grew. He alone had influence with the white soldiers. Consequently, he was finally able to round up the indemnity. On August 11, he and the Kiowa-Apache Chief Pacer handed over thirty-eight mules and one horse to the Fort Sill Agency. Together with two mules previously delivered, the amount required by Sherman had been returned. Tatum and Major G.W. Schofield, Tenth Cavalry, commanding Fort Sill while Colonel Grierson was in the field, accepted for the government.

Tatum was impressed with the care that had gone into selecting the animals. "They are a very good lot of mules," he

---

[6]Ibid., 362-65; Darlington, receipt for three mules and one pony, November 3, 1871, Letters Received.

[7]Soward to Tatum, September 19, 1871, Kiowa File.

wrote to Hoag, "some of them superior."[8] Still, he intended there should be no misunderstanding. The fact that the requisite number of animals had been gathered for return to Texas did not necessarily mean the slate was clean.

Reading from a prepared statement, Tatum told the chiefs:

> As the forty one mules stolen by Satanta and other Kiowas, have been delivered to me, then there will be nothing more done with the Kiowas, at present. I cannot tell whether the Govt. Officers at Washington will require anything more of them or not. It may be, that they will make further requirements of the Kiowas. I am not authorized to make a permanent treaty of peace. Eagle Heart, Fast Bear, or Big Bear, who accompanied Satanta in his late raid, will *not in the future* be recognized as Chiefs, but they will not be arrested unless the officers at Washington order their arrest. *Provided* the Kiowas make no more raids. If they should make another raid anywhere, the above named Chiefs, and leaders of the raiding party, whether Chiefs or not, will be liable to be arrested, and tried by Civil Law.

Furthermore, he said he would depose any chief who accompanied any future raiding party. Kicking Bird and Pacer would then nominate successors, subject to Tatum's approval.

Tatum concluded by saying the government wished peace and prosperity to all the tribes, and would make any reasonable effort to assist them. In turn, the government expected good behavior. "We are all brothers in the sight of God," he said, "and we desire you to live as brothers, and not as hungry wolves."

The Indians agreed to the conditions, and said they would have nominations the following day to replace Eagle Heart, Big Bear and Fast Bear. Then Kicking Bird spoke.

We intend to cease raiding and depredating on the white people

---

[8]Tatum to Hoag, August 12, 1871, Letters Received. Ironically, after the mules were returned to Henry Warren, two of them were found to have *US* brands and were confiscated from the embarrassed Warren as government property. See Hamilton, *Sentinel*, 202.

and hereafter follow the example of the Caddoe [*sic*] Indians, who have long been on the White mans road. As evidence of our good intentions we have brought in the mules as required of us. And now we want you to write a strong appeal to the officers at Washington for the release of Satanta & Big Tree, who we think have now suffered enough, and then everything will be right.[9]

Kicking Bird said all the Kiowas had returned to the reservation, and were camped along Buffalo Creek, near its confluence with the North Fork of the Red River. Pacer gave the location of the Kiowa-Apaches as being along the Washita, near the site of the 1868 massacre by Custer's men during the winter campaign.

Schofield and Tatum replied they would notify their superiors that the Indians had returned to their reservations and delivered the mules. They also forwarded the Indian request for the release of Satanta and Big Tree. Tatum recommended that the issue of rations to the Kiowas and Kiowa-Apaches resume immediately.[10]

Viewed in the light of events in Texas, the tension among the agency tribes was a footnote in the overall story of the Indian Trial. Yet while it lasted, it had the potential for a full-scale rising that easily could have soaked the plains in blood.

To some degree disaster was averted by apathy among the Southern Cheyennes. Kiowa hopes for an alliance with them never had any basis in reality. The Cheyenne leaders had a much firmer grip on their people than did their Kiowa counterparts, and support among the Cheyenne chiefs was never strong. Darlington's watchfulness, together with the rapport that Colonel Davidson established between the chiefs and the military caused any sympathy for the Kiowas to completely evaporate.

---

[9]Tatum to Hoag, August 12, 1871, Letters Received.
[10]Schofield to AAG, Department of the Missouri, August 12, 1871, ibid.

PART 4:   THE TRIAL

But the main factors in keeping the peace were the emergence of Kicking Bird as the dominant political force among the Kiowas, and the refusal of the Comanches to participate. Individual groups from both nations might raid as they please, but it was virtually impossible for the Kiowas to mount a general war without Comanche support.

So as Texas prepared to send Satanta and Big tree to prison, the plains grew quiet. But most of the raiders, including White Horse, Eagle Heart, and Maman-ti, were still on the loose. They bided their time, waiting for the appropriate moment. No one was more aware of this than Mackenzie. On the day he returned to Fort Richardson with Satanta and Big Tree in tow, he had written Sherman that the Kiowas and Comanches could never be pacified until they were "dismounted, and made to raise corn, &c." And to do this, soldiers would be needed from as far away as New Mexico and the Platte, as well as those from the immediate vicinity of the Indian Territory, Kansas and Texas.[11] In the long term, events would prove him right.

---

[11]Mackenzie to Sherman, June 15, 1871, in Sherman, Unofficial Correspondence.

CHAPTER 9
"What Is to be Done With These Indians?"

The trial was having an impact on the frontier. Shortly after
it ended, the grand jury of Montague County indicted White
Horse for the murder of Gottlieb Koozer. A letter was sent to
Grierson at Fort Sill, requesting the arrest of the chief and his
extradition to Texas. It was impossible to comply because
White Horse was at large. Still the indictment showed the
Texans were tired of the raids and were willing to use the legal
system to strike back if the government would not defend
them.[1]

In areas directly under the War Department, the military
was trying to defend them. But the "limited resources" cited in
Belknap's letter to the Weatherford citizen were limited
indeed. Mackenzie found it difficult to sweep the plains of
hostiles, but he was learning. The day of Satanta's trial,
Reynolds had approved an expedition to force the Kiowas
back to the reservation. He also wrote the War Department
that if this expedition failed, the government should consider
"a more general movement against the Indians this fall, or
winter...." Sherman concurred, but stipulated that Mackenzie
was not to cross from Texas into the Indian Territory unless

---

[1]Nye, *Carbine and Lance*, 150.

123

specifically invited by Grierson. In such cases, the latter officer would have overall command.[2]

Grierson did not see the urgency of the situation. He felt the arrest of the chiefs, the failure to gain allies for a rising and the subsequent emergence of Kicking Bird had substantially defused the situation. In fact, he and Jones told Tatum that they had never seen the Kiowas "so effectually subdued before." Tatum agreed. Convinced he had done the right thing in allowing the arrests, he wrote the Friends Committee, "It has probably saved the lives of many Texas citizens." He added, "He whom I endeavor to serve has, I believe, enlightened my understanding in times of need." The delivery of the mules for Henry Warren served as further proof of Indian good will.[3]

Huntsville is located deep in the forests of the east. Sam Houston owned a house there during one of his periodic retirements from public affairs, and considered the time spent there with his wife raising a family to be the happiest of his life. He returned there to die after he was deposed from the governorship for refusing to take an oath of allegiance to the Confederate States of America. An old and venerable state university is also located there.

But Huntsville's main industry was—and is—the state prison system. Here Satanta and Big Tree were received on November 2, 1871, and were registered as Numbers 2107 and 2108 respectively.[4] As they settled in, the contrast between the

[2]Reynolds to Mackenzie, July 6, 1871, "Official Correspondence," *Museum Journal* 9:35; Reynolds to AG USA, July 14, 1871, ibid., 9:37; Sherman to J.C. McCoy, ADC, July 29, 1871, ibid., 9:36. Sherman disliked Mackenzie and distrusted his ambition. Although he regarded the young colonel as an extremely competent field officer, he felt some control was needed to keep him in line. For a more complete look at Sherman's relations with Mackenzie and other "boy generals," see Hutton, *Phil Sheridan.*   [3]Tatum, *Red Brothers,* 122-25.

[4]Post returns show the prison detail left Fort Richardson on October 17, and returned on November 26. This would make seventeen days going and twenty-four returning, reasonable time for coach travel between Jacksboro and Huntsville in those days. The return trip would have been understandably longer, since the detachment would not have been so pressed for time. Details of the Indians' admission to Huntsville are in Huckabay, *Ninety-four Years,* 190; McConnell, *Five Years a Cavalryman,* 288-89, and the Texas Prison Papers.

Satanta and Big Tree in prison. *Texas State Library and Archive.*

two Indians was apparent. Satanta, well into late middle age, refused to adjust to his confinement. He was a warrior first and last, and without the freedom of the plains, life was pointless. He viewed the prison work program as particularly demeaning, and prison officials had trouble getting him to cooperate. Ultimately they left him alone, and Satanta worked when he wanted to, picking shucks or pulling wool for mattresses.[5]

A correspondent from *Scribner's Monthly*, a New York mag-

[5]Strong, *Frontier Days*, 22-23; Wilbarger, *Indian Depredations*, 573.

azine, visited the two chiefs in prison in 1873. Satanta, who had enthroned himself on a pile of oakum, stood up, gave the writer a firm handshake,

> and sat down, motioning to me to be seated with as much dignity and grace as though he were a monarch receiving a foreign ambassador....Although he is much more than 60 years old,[6] he hardly seemed 40, so erect, elastic, vigorous was he. When asked if he ever expected liberation, and what he would do if it should come, he responded, "Quien sabe?" [Who knows?] with the most stoical indifference. Big-tree was briskly at work plaiting a chair seat in another apartment and chewing tobacco vigorously. His face was clear cut and handsome, his coal black hair swept his shoulders, and he only paused to brush it back and give us a swift glance as we entered, then briskly plaited as before.[7]

Barely out of his teens, Big Tree realized he would spend the greater part of his life in a world controlled by whites. The best way to handle that was to get along with them. In the prison shops, he soon gained a reputation for weaving and installing more wicker bottoms into chairs than any other inmate.[8]

Not far from Huntsville, in Polk County, were the remnants of the Alabama and Coushatta tribes, eastern woodland groups who had moved to Texas under white pressure in the late eighteenth and early nineteenth centuries. These Indians had always been at peace with the whites, and in fact, had earned the gratitude of the state for sheltering refugees from Santa Anna's armies during the War of Independence. And as Colonel Reynolds, the departmental commander, noted, these tribes "subsist by their own labor."

Reynolds suggested the Alabama and Coushatta chiefs visit Satanta and Big Tree in prison. This, in turn, might lead to further contacts between the East Texas Indians and the Kiowas, which might encourage the latter tribe to try reserva-

---

[6] He was actually about fifty-six.
[7] *Scribner's Monthly* February 1874, 415, quoted in Mooney, *Calendar History*, 209.
[8] Wilbarger, *Indian Depredations*, 573.

tion life as an alternative to raiding. "Such intercourse with other wild Indians might possibly also result from this plan, if it should be deemed worthy of trial," he wrote.[9]

Why contact with the Alabamas and Coushattas should subdue the Kiowas, when years of regular councils with the Five Civilized Tribes in the Indian Territory had failed to do so was not explained. There is no record that Reynolds' plan was ever tried.

A few months after Satanta and Big Tree went to prison, Captain Wirt Davis and Company "F" of the Fourth Cavalry built a monument over the mass grave of the seven teamsters. Constructed by the Quartermaster's Department at Fort Richardson and hauled to the site in sections, it was a pyramid of oak painted with the memorial:

> Sacred to the memory of seven brave men killed by Indians at this place on Thurs. May 18 '71 while in discharge of their duty defending this train against 150 Comanche [sic] Indians. N.S. Long— Wagon master. J.S. Elliott, Sam Elliott, N.J. Baxter, Jas. Williams, John Mullins, Jesse Bowman, Teamsters.[10]

Despite outward appearances, the Kiowa problem was far from settled. Factious as always, the Kiowas were still divided into peace and war parties. Although the Comanches as a whole had refused to join a general rising, the Quahadi band of the tribe, under the brilliant, half-white War Chief Quanah Parker, continued to raid into Texas. Inspired by Quanah, White Horse and Lone Wolf encouraged the Kiowa war faction, which began regaining its prestige. The war faction remained relatively quiet through the remainder of 1871, watching as Mackenzie's summer campaign bogged down with conflicting government policies. The fall campaign was equally unsuccessful. The military spent those weeks on a wild

---

[9]Reynolds to AG USA, September, 20, 1871, Letters Received.
[10]Carter,*On the Border*, 103-04; text recorded in Kellogg, *Journal*, 150. Miner K. Kellogg saw the monument on September 9, 1872.

goose chase led by the Quahadis, and when the year ended the Indians were still firmly in control of the plains, raiding with impunity as far as Weatherford and beyond.

Following Quanah's example, White Horse decided that 1872 would be his year. In April, he joined Big Bow in leading a war party that attacked a wagon train at Howard's Wells, on the road between San Antonio and El Paso. Seventeen teamsters were killed and the train was looted. A patrol of Ninth Cavalry from Fort Concho discovered the massacre and followed the Indians to their camp. The Kiowas held them off until nightfall, then withdrew.

Meanwhile, White Horse's younger brother, Kom-pai-te, left behind because White Horse considered him to young for raiding, had joined a party of Comanches heading into Texas. They attacked a group of surveyors near Fort Belknap, and Kom-pai-te was killed. Learning of his brother's death, White Horse organized a vengeance raid and, on June 9, 1872, attacked the Abel Lee home near Fort Griffin. Lee, his wife, and an eight-year-old daughter were killed, while two other daughters and a son were carried off into captivity.[11]

The situation reached the point where Brigadier General C.C. Augur, who had recently replaced Reynolds as commander of the Department of Texas, wrote to General Sheridan, "The cavalry from Fort Richardson has been almost constantly employed for the past month in chasing bands of indian [sic] depredators in the northern counties of Texas." He added the Indians were from the Fort Sill Reservation, and said evidence "leaves no doubt they are Kiowas...."

> The question then is, what is to be done with these indians? The popular panacea in cases of hostile indians--of putting them on a reservation and feeding them, is not applicable in this case, as they are, or are supposed to be, already on one, and have been for years,

---

[11]Nye, *Carbine and Lance*, 152-54; Lieutenant, E.C. Gilbreath to Post Adjutant, Fort Griffin, June 11, 1871, in "Official Correspondence," *Museum Journal*, 9:77-78.

where they are fed and cared for by the Government. Some other remedy must be prescribed."[12]

Sheridan concurred. In his endorsement, he vented his fury on Colonel Hazen, the former superintendent of the Southern Indian Military District, who was publicly castigating the government for not punishing the Indians.

"He seems to have forgotten...that when I had my sabers drawn to do it, that he pronounced them in the name of the Peace Commission friendly," Sheridan remarked.[13]

The government was now divided into even more factions than the Kiowas. Members of the same branch of service, supposedly operating toward the same goal, were not speaking to each other. Meanwhile, the government faced a crisis on the plains. While not a full-scale uprising, the raids had escalated into a minor guerrilla war. Tatum estimated that fully one-fourth of the Kiowas were off the reservation, raiding with the Quahadis. By June, the Kiowas had not drawn rations for five months even though they normally did so regardless of hostilities. None of the Comanches were coming in regularly. On June 22, Mackenzie reported, "There have been more depredations lately than ever before—four murders in the last week that are really true and since, nine more reported, of the truth of which I am not yet convinced."[14]

While the government fretted, the Civilized Tribes appointed a delegation to meet with the Kiowas, to try to convince them to stop raiding, and invite them to a general

---

[12]Augur to Sheridan, June 10, 1872, ibid., 9:80.

[13]Sheridan, endorsement of June 19, 1872, to Augur's letter of June 10, 1872, ibid., 9:82. Sheridan was referring to his winter campaign of 1868-69, in which Hazen had given a safe conduct to Satanta and Lone Wolf. Although Sheridan always believed the Kiowas were largely responsible for the outbreaks that led to that campaign, they had only a minor role and for the most part kept to themselves until they were attacked. See Stan Hoig, *The Battle of the Washita.*

[14]Tatum, *Red Brothers*, 132; Mackenzie to AAG Department of Texas, June 22, 1872, RG 391 Series 757, Fourth Cavalry Expedition Records, Letters and Endorsements Sent and Orders Issued.

council at the abandoned military post of Fort Cobb, on July 22, 1872. Tatum was against it. The Kiowas had done without rations for a long time. He felt that if he held out a little longer, they would surrender their prisoners without demanding a ransom. But pressure from the superintendent's office caused him to agree to the council.

When the Kiowas arrived, White Horse said he was not interested in peace and would continue raiding as he pleased. Lone Wolf had a list of demands for the return of the Lee children. First, he said Satanta and Big Tree were to be released from prison. All military posts were to be removed from the Indian Territory, and the reservation would be extended from the Rio Grande to the Missouri.

The more realistic Civilized Tribes observed that if the Kiowas did not return the prisoners and settle down, the government would retaliate. Tatum was not present because his wife was ill, but Kicking Bird sent him a private message that he opposed Lone Wolf's demands, and would try to use his influence to secure the release of the prisoners. Cyrus Beede, Superintendent Hoag's chief clerk, urged him to turn them over to the agency immediately.

Ultimately, the Kiowas agreed to liberate the prisoners, send a delegation to Washington, and comply with various other government demands. In return, the federal government promised to free Satanta and Big Tree no later than March 1873.[15] Once again, the United States was illegally infringing on the sovereignty of Texas by attempting to nullify the sentence of the state court.

About a month after the Fort Cobb council, the Lee girls were delivered to Agent Jonathan Richards at the Wichita Agency. He issued rations to the Kiowas and hired Caddo

---

[15]Tatum, *Red Brothers*, 125-26; G.W. Greyson to the President and Secretary of the Interior, May 1873, in Day and Winfrey, *Texas Indian Papers*, 341.

George Washington to take the girls and their Kiowa escorts to Fort Sill. When they reached their own agency, the Indians told Tatum that the girls came alone because their brother John was too sick to travel. The girls, however, insisted he was in good health and had wanted to accompany them, even though they initially did not know where they were being taken.

Tatum refused to even consider paying a ransom for the return of the girls.

> I told them that paying for them was an encouragement to steal more, and that they should not have a dollar, and that they could have no more rations until the boy was brought. These girls were the first captives ever recovered from the Kiowas without paying from $100 to $1,500 for each one.

Although Tatum would have preferred having all the surviving children back, he at least had the girls. They were turned over to the agency school while he contacted relatives in Texas. An adult brother came for them and was at the school on September 30 when the Indians delivered John Lee. Within a few days they are on their way back home.

Meanwhile, the Kiowa representatives were beginning to balk at the idea of going to Washington. Finally, it was agreed that if they went they would be allowed to see Satanta and Big Tree en route. Lieutenant Robert Carter was ordered to take "E" Company of the Fourth Cavalry to Dallas, where he would receive the prisoners and convey them in double irons to the MKT railhead at Atoka in the Indian Territory. The train rolled into Dallas at 8 a.m. September 9, and the soldiers saw the familiar figure of Satanta through the coach window. Legirons clanking, he and Big Tree were brought down to the platform under heavy guard and turned over to the army. Soldiers surrounded them, pushed back the crowd of onlookers and hurried off to guard tents in the military camp. Carter was anxious to be out of Dallas, since armed cowboys and gun-slingers constantly hung around the camp.

The road from Dallas to Atoka was familiar country to Satanta, who had raided through it for many years. Often on the trail, he would point out something to Big Tree and begin reminiscing. They reached Atoka without incident, where Carter coordinated the remainder of the trip with Captain H. E. Alvord, who was escorting the Kiowa delegation. Alvord's group left first for St. Louis, with Satanta and Big Tree following in a later train to avoid contact with the other chiefs.

The two groups met at noon September 19, at the Everett House in St. Louis. Alvord was there, along with Hoag and other dignitaries. Satanta told the assembled chiefs that he was being treated well, and urged them to stop raiding into Texas. After the visit, he and Big Tree were returned to Huntsville, while the others went on to Washington.[16] There, again, the Indians were given to understand that pardon of the prisoners was being considered, in return for good behavior of the tribe.[17] Those who had once argued for a life sentence as preferable to hanging were now striving for unconditional release. This was subject to the consent of Governor Davis, but to the politicians in Washington that was a forgone conclusion. After all, although Davis had been given a new term in a sham election, he was essentially a Reconstruction appointee, and depended on Washington to stay in power.

The Friends Committee and other Indian advocates were jubilant. Ever the diplomat, Satanta was playing on their sympathies and their gullibility. He was now representing himself as principal chief of the Kiowas and several other nations in the southwestern Indian Territory. He assured the idealists that if he was released, he would keep the tribes under control. This was a promise he could not keep even within his own

[16]Carter, *On the Border*, 349-72; Nye, *Carbine and Lance*, 160; Pate, "Mackenzie," 115; Tatum, *Red Brothers*, 126-29.   [17]Delano to Davis, March 22, 1873, Kiowa File.

tribe, and certainly not within the others. And it was a promise that would eventually ruin him.

Tatum was not bluffed. The gentle Quaker had lost all his illusions in the harsh realities of the plains. He realized that Satanta did not have the authority he claimed, and would not have used it in any case. He also knew that Kiowa values were different from Anglo-Saxon values. Release of Satanta and Big Tree would not be taken as a sign of magnanimity and strength. It would be taken as a sign of weakness—that the unending raids had forced the white government to bend to the Kiowa will.

"My judgment was to send some more of the leading raiders to the penitentiary, and in that way stop their unprovoked hostility," he wrote. When his committee asked his opinion on the release, he replied that it would be "very wrong."

Tatum's status with the committee and with Hoag and Beede was already shaky because he had allowed the chiefs to be arrested in the first place. As Friend William Nicholson wrote him, following a committee meeting in New York, "There was evidently some concern on the part of several of the Committee lest thou complicate thyself with military matters to such an extent as to compromise our religious principles, whilst there was also very evidently a prevailing feeling of sympathy with thee in thy very trying position."

Now that the Friends Committee openly advocated release of Satanta and Big Tree, the rift was much more serious. Tatum knew trouble was brewing on the agency and doubted he would be able to control his Indian charges much longer. The release of the two Kiowas might very well make it impossible. Convinced that further efforts on his part were futile, he sent in his resignation effective March 31, 1873. Misplaced idealism among higher authorities had driven off one of the most competent men on the plains.[18]

---

[18]Tatum, *Red Brothers*, 131-33; Nicholson to Tatum, August 22, 1871, Kiowa File.

Kiowa Agency, Fort Sill, 1872. Leo. Smith,
clerk; Mrs. Smith; Henry Lamb, cook; Mrs.
Tatum; L. Tatum, Agent. Photo by W.S. Soule.
*Archives & Manuscripts Division of the
Oklahoma Historical Society.*

Part 5: The Parole

CHAPTER 10
"You Nor Your Sub-Agents Are to Make Any Promises to the Indians"

If the pacifists fared badly in 1872, the final quarter of the year was a good one for the army. On September 29, Mackenzie stormed a Comanche camp on the North Fork of the Red River, destroying 262 lodges and taking over 120 prisoners, mostly women and children, with some wounded men. One member of Mackenzie's party, a teamster named José Carrión, recognized some of the Indian mules as having belonged to the wagon train destroyed at Howard's Wells.[1] The prisoners were taken to Fort Concho, where General Augur recommended they be held until all white captives and government livestock were returned.

The action was a profound shock to the hostiles. Accustomed to dictating conditions for release of white hostages, they found themselves forced to ask for terms for their own families. Fort Concho was too far south for a raid to free so many people, and Mackenzie's attack forced some sort of immediate solution. The government offered it by promising to free Satanta and Big Tree in exchange for good behavior. Perhaps, they reasoned, this could be extended to the prisoners at Fort Concho as well.

---

[1]Mackenzie to AAG. Department of Texas, October 12, 1872, RG 391. Series 757, Fourth Cavalry Expedition Records.

The Kiowas were less concerned than the Comanches because very few of their people had been captured, and they seemed to feel no sense of urgency over the two chiefs. They held back from raiding for a different reason. Their delegation had returned from Washington awed by the power of the whites. Those who scoffed at the stories were convinced when Thomas Battey, who taught school at Kicking Bird's camp, presented a magic lantern show of the great cities of the east. So the plains grew quiet as the Indians awaited new developments. For the first time, the Comanches moved their winter camp in close to the agency, and stolen livestock began filtering back to military custody at Fort Sill.[2]

By February 1873, the government was less concerned with raids from the Indian Territory than depredations along the Rio Grande by Indians hiding in Mexico. Consequently, President Grant and General Sherman decided the Fourth Cavalry would be more useful on that frontier, while units of the Seventh Cavalry could hold Fort Richardson.[3] The following month, Interior Secretary Delano wrote Governor Davis, "The Kiowas having conducted themselves in a manner to meet the approbation of the Department, it is believed the time has arrived when their expectations in relation to the release of the prisoners may be properly realized." He then asked Davis to pardon Satanta and Big Tree on April 15, "provided your judgment in all respects approves the pardon."[4]

In Lawrence, Hoag assumed the pardon would occur. On

---

[2]Schofield to AAG, Department of Texas, January 17, 1873, "Official Correspondence," *Museum Journal* 9:159-60; Battey, *Life and Adventures*, 257-58; Haley, *Buffalo War*, 39; Nye, *Carbine and Lance*, 164.

[3]Although long associated with Lieutenant Colonel George Armstrong Custer, the Seventh was scattered throughout the frontier during most of the first 10 years of its history. In fact, the Little Bighorn campaign of 1876 was the first time the entire regiment was assembled together since its organization.

[4]Sherman to Augur, February 5, 1873, "Official Correspondence," *Museum Journal*, 9:161-62; Delano to Davis, March 22, 1873, Kiowa File.

March 28, his clerk, Beede, met with the Kiowas and Comanches to discuss "the matter of delivery" of Satanta and Big Tree, as well as to consider the Comanche prisoners at Fort Concho. Among other things, the superintendent wanted a general council at the Kiowa Agency when the two chiefs were delivered, to get maximum effect from the action. By this means, he intended to obtain "renewed pledges of friendship and peace from all the tribes of the Southwest." Just why he expected these pledges to be any different from the ones given previously was not explained.

Hoag was growing uneasy. He wanted the Indians kept in custody until they reached Fort Sill for two reasons. First, there was the public relations coup he hoped to score by freeing them in the presence of the Kiowa nation. Second, Delano had made no provision for their safety. If they simply were discharged at Huntsville, Hoag doubted they would live long enough to reach the reservation. If they died en route, he said, "serious consequences might follow."[5]

Time would be needed to arrange the council and security for the two prisoners, so Hoag asked Davis to delay the release until April 20. He suggested escorting them to Fort Sill, where the new agent, J.M. Haworth, would take custody and deliver them to the council. Finally, he asked for "a delegation of prominent and leading men of the state of Texas, be also in attendance, that the Indians may have the benefit of their council as well as that of this office."

Suddenly, negotiations were brought to a standstill by a totally unrelated event over a thousand miles to the west. For four months, the army had been fighting the Modoc Indians in the lava fields of northern California. The desperate struggle of the Modocs in a war they had not provoked won

---

[5]Hoag to Edward P. Smith, commissioner of Indian Affairs, April 9, 1873; Hoag to Davis, April 9, 1873, both in Kiowa File.

national admiration. Because public opinion supported the Modocs, the military commander, Brigadier General Edward Canby, was authorized to head a three-man delegation to negotiate an end to the war with the Modoc Chief Captain Jack. Spurred on by a medicine man's prophecy, Captain Jack met the unarmed Canby and another white delegate on April 11 and assassinated them.[6]

Public support turned to outrage. Three days after the murders, Delano, with the full concurrence of President Grant, telegraphed Davis withdrawing his request for pardon of the two Kiowas. On April 18, he followed it with a letter of explanation, saying

> In consequence of the excited condition of public sentiment in regard to Indian Affairs growing out of our recent difficulties with the Modocs, added to other reasons therefor [sic], the President and myself had concluded that it is not best at present at least to pardon Satanta and Big Tree.

The "other reasons therefor" were none other than Sherman, who had written Canby's successor urging the "utter extermination" of the Modocs. He was in no mood to hear of a pardon for any Indian.[7]

It fell on the teacher, Thomas Battey, to tell the Kiowas, and in doing so, he very nearly became the proverbial messenger killed for bringing bad tidings. He found the Kiowas and several other plains tribes preparing for the annual Sun Dance. The chiefs were in council considering whether go to war over Satanta and Big Tree. When he told them the prisoners would not be released, they were surprised, then confused, then angry. The majority believed Battey should be killed, and the women

---

[6]The Modoc War is covered in detail in Wellman, *Death in the Desert*, 103-27.

[7]Delano to Davis, May 27, 1873, Kiowa File. Captain Jack surrendered on June 1, 1873, and was tried, condemned and hanged along with three of his men. Unlike the Kiowas, there was no public outcry on his behalf, even though his overall moral position vis-a-vis the whites was much more solid than that of Satanta or Big Tree. See Wellman, *Death in the Desert*, 124-27.

138

and children hidden in the Staked Plains of the Texas Panhandle, after which separate parties would launch simultaneous attacks on the border settlements of Texas, New Mexico and Kansas.

Battey's nerve held, and he argued for time. He told them he had written the commissioner, pointing out that the Kiowas had maintained the peace, and for that reason, Satanta and Big Tree should go free. He urged them to wait for a reply, saying that when the government learned the true situation, it might release the prisoners after all. Kicking Bird backed him, and the chiefs agreed. Meanwhile, Battey would remain hostage until they were released.[8]

Reaction to the Modoc War worried the Confederated Tribes as they gathered once again in Okmulgee. They sympathized with the Kiowas. With or without legal authority, the federal government had promised the release of the chiefs. As G.W. Greyson, council secretary, wrote to Grant and Delano, the Kiowas

> cannot understand why the Government should exact rigid compliance with every promise on their part and at the same time practice non-observance on its own part—Nor can they comprehend or understand why they are practically held responsible for the doings of the Modoc on the Pacific Coast, of whom they have probably never heard. They have declared their readiness to bind themselves to the Govt of the United States and the Confederated Tribes jointly—to take a position between the two, clinging to the hands of each. What more can they do to assure the Government of their pacific intentions?"[9]

The council itself passed a resolution calling on Hoag as its

---

[8]Battey's situation is described in Nye, *Carbine and Lance*, 166-67. In his own narrative, (*Life and Adventures*, 156-61), Battey did not mention his detention. Instead, he quotes a letter he sent to Agent Haworth explaining the Kiowa position and describing the various ways in which the tribe had sought to comply with the government's edicts. Haworth forwarded the letter to Commissioner Edward Smith.

[9]Greyson to the president and secretary of the interior, May 1873, Day and Winfrey, *Texas Indian Papers*, 340.

president "to congratulate the Kiowas, Cheyennes and other Tribes of the Plains, for the laudable manner in which they have conducted themselves in the maintenance of friendly relations with the U.S. as well as among themselves." The resolution also promised the council's "every effort" in securing the release of Satanta and Big Tree. It was signed by forty-seven delegates representing ten tribes. Hoag and Greyson also signed.

These tribal statements were not as naive as they sounded. The council was very much aware that the "friendly relations" were maintained by military force. In fact, the resolution specifically warned the plains tribes that the safety and survival of the Indians as a race depended on keeping peace with the federal government.[10]

Eventually, the Modoc furor cooled down, and on May 27, Secretary Delano was again in a position to urge the release of the Kiowa chiefs. Hoag wrote Agent Haworth, "It now appears the pressure bro[ough]t. to bear on the Pres[iden]t & Secy. by the public, growing out of the Modoc War—and opposition from Genl. Sherman—has been overcome by better councils." He added he hoped "the Governor will yield to the request and that thou wilt manage with all possible prudence for the maintenance of peace."[11]

It seemed like everybody was getting into the act. Edward Smith, the Indian commissioner, advocated release of Satanta and Big Tree, and if that wasn't possible, release of the prisoners at Fort Concho. He was more concerned about the latter group because they were being held at federal expense, the government even supplying forage for their horses, and their liberation would relieve the United States of a substantial financial burden. Whether they were sent to Fort Sill under

---

[10]General Council of the Indian Territory, Resolution relating to the Kiowas[,] Cheyennes and other tribes of the Plains, Kiowa File.

[11]Delano to Davis, May 27, 1873; Hoag to Haworth, June 3, 1873, both in Kiowa File.

military escort or turned out on their own from Fort Concho was of no concern to Smith as long as his office was rid of them.[12] Already out on a limb, the federal position was rapidly becoming absurd.

In the midst of all these discussions, Smith raised the previously ignored point that Satanta and Big Tree were state prisoners, and that the final decision rested with the governor of Texas.[13] Bureaucrats in Washington and Lawrence, who had previously spoken confidently of a pardon, now began discussing what it might take to convince Davis to release them under any condition.

Meanwhile, at Fort Sill, the Indians were becoming restless. Lone Wolf, who was beginning to emerge as the undisputed leader of the war faction, was trying to keep things under control, but there were limits to what he or any other ranking chief could do. The release was a point of honor rather than an urgent necessity, and it was now well into the season normally given to raiding. On June 3, Hoag wrote Richards at Anadarko:

> The Secy. [of the] Interior (President concurring) addressed an urgent letter to Gov. of Texas on 29th ult. for the release of the Kiowa chiefs, giving the best of reasons therefor [sic] *I want every effort to be made to maintain peace & quiet hoping the time is near when the prisoners will be restored* [italics added].

In a similar frame of mind, Delano told Commissioner Smith to advise Haworth to assure the Indians that negotiations were still underway, "and to do all in his power to preserve their confidence, and await patiently the necessary delay."[14]

The situation was extremely touchy. Hoag notified

---

[12]Smith to Delano, May 22, 1873, Day and Winfrey, *Texas Indian Papers*, 338-39.

[13]Smith to Haworth, June 26, 1873, quoted in Battey, *Life and Adventures*, 160-61.

[14]Hoag to Richards, June 3, 1873; Delano to Commissioner of Indian Affairs, July 11, 1873, both Kiowa File.

141

Haworth that Smith had asked for a council with the Kiowas on October 1. It would be attended by Delano, as well as Davis and other Texas officials, "at which time the Indians may be encouraged to *hope* for the release of their captive chiefs....

> Thou wilt impress upon Lone Wolf and other chiefs the responsibility of their present position. If they fail at this time to control their young men, and to maintain friendly relations with the Government and people of the United States including Texas *all will be lost* and their friends who are working continually for the restoration of their chiefs will have little to hope for in the future.

Smith and Hoag hoped the Kiowas would be mollified by being able to meet Davis and Satanta on their own territory, as well as express their views to "Washington" without leaving home. This way, also, it would be unnecessary for another delegation to travel to the capital, something that always made the Kiowas nervous.[15]

Abruptly, things began falling into place. On June 10, the Fort Concho prisoners arrived at Fort Sill. "This has been a day of rejoicing," Josiah Butler wrote. "Some of the Indians wept for very joy....The prisoners all remained together until after the council this afternoon. I saw several meetings of husbands and wives and of parents and children; some cried, some laughed and some mourned over departed loved ones."[16]

Six weeks later, during a visit to Iowa, Hoag received a telegram from B.R. Cowan, acting secretary of the interior in Delano's absence. Davis was in Washington and had agreed to send Satanta and Big Tree to Fort Sill under guard, upon his return home.[17]

---

[15]Hoag to Haworth, July 15, 1873, ibid.   [16]Butler, "Pioneer School Teaching," 527-28.
[17]B.R. Cowan to Hoag, July 30, 1873, quoted in letter from Beede to Haworth, August 5, 1873, Kiowa File.

142

When word reached the Kiowas, Battey was released. Living under the constant threat of death had made him a nervous wreck. Agent Haworth, however, was not enthusiastic about having Satanta and Big Tree back at his agency as prisoners two months before the council was to convene. Cyrus Beede encouraged him to try. He told Haworth that if the Kiowas remained under control during that time, it might go far toward their release. Although he said he would hesitate to give them too much assurance, Satanta would be able to meet with the other chiefs and advise the tribe through them. This would encourage them to hold on until the council convened.[18]

At this point, the government made an incredible blunder. Apparently at the instigation of the War Department, a survey of the reservation was begun. The Kiowas were appalled. Given their superstitious nature, they saw nothing but evil in the sight of white men setting up stakes, running lines and looking through tripod-mounted glasses. Measuring could also mean counting, and there was a deadly taboo against being counted. Even the more sophisticated among them, who recognized the survey for what it was, were frightened. This could mean the government was now planning to divide their land for settlement.[19]

Haworth fired off a letter to Colonel Davidson, now commanding Fort Sill, with a copy to Beede at the Central Superintendency in Lawrence, asking for a postponement. Beede endorsed it and sent it to Washington with a request for postponement on behalf of the Superintendent's Office. Acting Secretary Cowan acknowledged Haworth's report of the "restless feeling" the survey caused among the Kiowas. However, he replied it would continue until it was determined whether

---

[18]Beede to Haworth, ibid.; Nye, *Carbine and Lance,*, 167.
[19]Nye, *Carbine and Lance,* 165; Haley, *Buffalo War,* 39.

the arrival of Satanta and Big Tree at Fort Sill calmed the
Indians to a point that would make postponement or cancel-
lation of the survey unnecessary.[20]

The Indians were nearing the breaking point. Small bands
of raiders were now slipping in and out of the reservation. One
group killed a surveyor near the Red River. During the latter
part of August, Davidson led a scout through the entire area,
which convinced him that the reservation once again was a
haven for marauders.[21] Haworth had already sent the newly-
freed Battey to Lawrence with a verbal message for Hoag to
come to Fort Sill and personally assess the situation as soon as
possible. The superintendent was swamped with work and so
telegraphed Washington:

> A special messenger has just arrived from the Kiowa Agency and
> requests an immediate visit from me.
> Shall I tell him that the survey will be postponed, and what other
> encouragement shall I give them[?]

Cowan replied:

> War Department has ordered escort to convey Kiowa chiefs to
> Fort Sill. Will not this satisfy Indians without withdrawing survey-
> ing party[?] Answer immediately.

It seemed incredible that the officials in Washington could
not understand the problems the agents faced. Frustrated,
Hoag cabled back that a survey on the reservation itself was
neither practicable nor safe. He said it was impossible for
Haworth to explain it in any way that would satisfy the Indians.

---

[20]Beede to Haworth, August, 5, 1873; Cowan to Haworth, August 8, 1873, both in
Kiowa File. Haworth and Davidson disliked each other. Haworth was a firm advocate of the
Peace Policy, and never acquired Tatum's realism. He had an orthodox Quaker's adversion to
the army, and his first act as agent was to dismiss Tatum's military police force. Conversely,
Davidson did not share Grierson's belief in the Peace Policy and distrusted the Indians. See
Nye, *Carbine and Lance.* 165-67.
[21]Nye, *Carbine and Lance,* 167-68.

Hoag was having problems from another quarter as well. Davis was not going to surrender his state's sovereignty gracefully. He had lived in Texas in 1838, and had a long career in public service. Despite his postwar Radicalism, he was no federal lackey, and he understood the situation on the frontier as well as anyone. When Hoag inquired of him as to the date Satanta and Big Tree would be sent to Fort Sill, the governor replied:

> The Indian Chiefs await an escort to take them to Fort Sill when they will be under the controll [*sic*] of the military to await our proposed conference. It is expecially [*sic*] understood that *you nor your sub-agents are to make any promises to the Indians in regard to any action to be had about these chiefs* [italics added].[22]

Not content with that, Davis wrote Colonel Davidson with a copy to Hoag:

> Because the Tribes to which these Chiefs belong, have, as I am informed, unwarrantably [*sic*] been led to misunderstand the conditions under which I have concluded to pardon and release them, I will be obliged to you to give the Chiefs as well as their Tribes, to understand distinctly, that they are to accept no promises touching such release, as binding on me, which they do not have from me in person or in writing.

The governor was convinced the Kiowas and Comanches were raiding in Texas despite the claims of their agents, and that this had been occurring more or less continually. As for the agents' opinion that the tribes would go to war if Davis did not relent, he said a general war would be no worse than the current situation, and he would not yield to threats.

> I know the Indian character well enough to be aware that this will but open the door to endless demands. It is better to have this mattered settled at once.[23]

---

[22]Copies of all these exchanges are contained in a letter from Hoag to Haworth, August 12, 1873, Kiowa File.
[23]David to Davidson, August 14, 1873, ibid.

Hoag was genuinely offended by the governor's tone. "It might be inferred from Gov. Davis's telegram that unauthorized promises had been made to the Kiowas—which is unwarranted," he complained to Haworth.[24] For some reason he still had not completely grasped that only the State of Texas could legally release Satanta and Big Tree. Thus the various statements he had made earlier in the year, in anticipation of a pardon, were unauthorized even though he had made them on virtual guarantee by federal officials. The United States simply did not have the authority.

In late August, a military detachment went to Huntsville to pick up Satanta and Big Tree and take them to Fort Sill, where they were to be "held securely guarded" until Davis and Delano could come to an agreement about them. They arrived at Sill on September 4, and were placed in the guardhouse. Big Tree's brother, Dangerous Eagle, happened to be at the agency, and Haworth took him to the post where he was allowed a visit. When it ended, Dangerous Eagle jumped on his pony and headed for the Kiowa camps at full gallop.[25]

The Indians were not exactly certain what would happen. Big Bow was convinced that Satanta would be taken to Washington. If that was the case, he told agency officials he would restrain the young warriors from further raids into Texas, and would follow the White Man's Road. Once Satanta was released, he said they would settle down and behave themselves.[26]

As the Kiowas pondered the future, Davis found himself under pressure from another quarter. Raiders had struck in Jack County again. Throughout late August and early September, roving bands swept through the county, sometimes

---

[24]Hoag to Haworth, August 12, 1873, ibid.

[25]Chauncy McKeever, AAG, Department of Texas, to Commanding Officer, Fort Sill, August 23, 1873; Haworth to Richards, September 4, 1873, both in Kiowa File.

[26]Notes taken during issue day, untitled papers dated September 1873, ibid.

hitting within half a mile of Fort Richardson. Between 150 and two hundred horses and mules were stolen. About 8 a.m. September 13, Indians attacked Howell Walker, his little son, Henry, and Mortimer Stevens, who were deer hunting about seven miles southwest of Jacksboro. Stevens held out until the Walkers both were killed, then escaped into the thickets. He told the coroner there were about thirty-seven Indians, nine of whom appeared to be armed with Spencer rifles, and the others with revolvers, both indicating government issue. The mutilated bodies of the Walkers were found the following day along with Spencer cartridge cases. The coroner's jury ruled death by Indian attack and noted evidence showed the murderers to be reservation Indians from Fort Sill.[27]

"Public sentiment here is *intense*," one local citizen wrote the governor after the attack. "The only hope the Frontiersmen now have left, is that you can induce the U.S. Government to adopt *Stringent measures* that will effectually remedy these outrages and *Compel* the Indians to remain on their reservation. If you can effect this, it will make every frontiersman, your *friend*, personally, *politically*, but if Satanta and Big Tree are given up, *without adequate Security* for the protection on the frontier, the Republican Party is *defeated*—and *you* will be *Unjustly censured*."[28]

Davis was in a no-win situation. It would have been hard for anyone to find a friend or a neutral party, but the embattled governor found one. This was H.E. Alvord, the officer who had handled the Kiowa visit to St. Louis and Washington. He had since left the army and was now living in New England. Because of his frontier experience, Commissioner Smith had invited him to the conference. He was unable to attend, but had some valuable advice and encouragement for Davis.

[27]Day and Winfrey, *Texas Indian Papers*, entry 221, 432-48.
[28]Louis J. Valentine to Davis, September 14, 1873, ibid., 342-44.

To begin with, Alvord indicated that guarantees had been made to the Kiowas without first consulting the governor, perhaps to back him into a corner and force the issue. And he suspected the entire scheme had originated in Hoag's office in Lawrence. To counter this, he said Davis should throw responsibility back on those who had made the promises without his consent.

Additionally, he advised Davis to insist on "the *only safe* interpreters in the country, Horace P. Jones and Philip McCuster [McCusker]." He said Jones and McCusker had been banned by the Quakers, who considered their personal lives morally objectionable. But he pointed out their integrity as interpreters was beyond reproach and the Indians trusted them.[29]

Armed with this information and Alvord's encouragement, Davis prepared to meet his adversaries—red and white.

[29]Alvord to Davis, September 22, 1873, ibid., 348-49.

CHAPTER 11

"Texas Has Control of This Matter Entirely"

The preliminaries got underway on the military post at Fort Sill on October 4, with Davis, Commissioner Smith, Hoag and his agents on one side, and various Kiowa chiefs on the other. The question was where the actual conference would take place. Neither side trusted the other. Davis insisted the meeting be held at the post because he wanted to be under military protection. But the Kiowas remembered that the last time they had met there, three of their chiefs were arrested. Finally, the Indians gave in and agreed to meet on the post two days hence.[1]

To be certain the Indians understood his position before discussions began, Davis sent them written notice of his conditions. He told them he had consulted with Smith, the agents and Davidson, had stated his terms, and believed the Indians could comply with them if they really wanted peace. He also cautioned them that the terms were his as governor, and did not come from the other officials. "If they are not complied with, it will be better for the people of Texas, who are sufferers by the bad conduct of the Comanche & Kiowa, to have open war and settle this matter at once," he said.[2]

---

[1]Davidson to AAG, Department of Texas, October 8, 1873, RG 94 4447 AGO 1873; Nye, *Carbine and Lance*, 169. Because so many of Fort Sill's activities were interrelated with problems in Texas, jurisdiction over the post had been shifted from General Pope in the Department of the Missouri to General Augur in the Department of Texas.

[2]Letter from E.J. Davis, October 5, 1873, Day and Winfrey, *Texas Indian Papers*, 349-50.

The council convened under an awning in front of Davidson's office on Monday, October 6. The Indian delegation
included chiefs of the Kiowas, Comanches, Kiowa-Apaches,
Wichitas and Caddos, the latter two tribes present as
observers. Satanta's son, Tsa'l-au-te, rode up on a horse that
one of Davis' aides recognized as having been stolen from him.
However, he remained silent. The federal government was
represented by Hoag, Agents Haworth, John D. Miles and
Richards, and Commissioner Smith. Davidson detailed two of
his own officers to keep a "full and correct record" for General
Sherman. He also took the precaution of having the entire
garrison in quarters, officers on hand, and one company of
cavalry saddled in the stables in case a disturbance broke out.[3]
    Smith opened the proceedings with a few brief sentences
stressing honesty and goodwill, then gave the floor to Davis,
who began:

> People of the Comanche and Kiowa, I have brought back Satanta
> and Big Tree. They are here and we all see them. They were prison-
> ers to the Texans, and they [the Texans] could have taken their lives,
> but did not. I have come here because the people of Texas have been
> suffering a long time. I want to have peace if possible. We are at
> peace with all others of the Territory, and want peace with the Kiowa
> if we can. I have come here to make my talk as to what the Texans
> want. I will hear your talk and then tell them what the Texans want
> them to do, so that they can consider whether they want peace or
> war with Texas. Satanta and Big Tree can tell them what they have
> seen in Texas and how they were treated. They will make their talk,
> and then we will hear what the Kiowa have to say. I will then make
> my talk.[4]

    [3]Davidson to AAG, Department of Texas, October 8, 1873, RG 94 4447 AGO 1873;
Nye, *Carbine and Lance*, 169.
    [4]Day and Winfrey, *Texas Indian Papers*, 350. The dialogue was recorded as it was happen-
ing, with notes taken rapidly and haphazardly. No effort was made toward correct punctuation,
capitalization or spelling. Thus the original copy on file in Austin (published in the *Texas
Indian Papers*) makes difficult reading, although when spoken it sound logical. In view of this,
I have modernized the capitalization and punctuation to make it flow more smoothly. No

It was hard to tell whether the governor was bluffing. He had been first placed in office by U.S. military authorities and continued in office at the will and pleasure of the federal government. Yet Reconstruction was winding down in Texas, and he hoped to retain his position in a legitimate election. Beyond that, he had spent most of his adult life in Texas and understood the mood of the people. They were ready to fight, with or without the United States, and it is quite possible that he was ready to lead them.

As Davis' words sank in, Satanta's aged father, To-quodle-kaip-tau, stood and approached Davis. He was no longer interested in points of honor or white-Indian politics. He came as a father to plead for his son. Davis apparently realized this, for he sat quietly and allowed the old man to place his hands on his head and invoke a blessing. When that was finished, To-quodle-kaip-tau said, "I am an old and poor man, and I ask that you take pity on me and give me my own. You have your squaws and your children. I love my children as well as you love yours, and I want my son."

His mood was reflected by Satanta himself. Two years in Huntsville had mellowed him. He was as clever as ever, but much of the real fight was gone. He wanted to be free of the prison walls and back on his own plains. Motioning to his striped convict clothing, he said in Comanche, "Strip these things off of me that I have worn in prison. Turn me over to the Kiowa, and I will live on the white man's road forever. Turn me over to my people, and they will do as the white man wants them."

---

other changes have been made. At times there are third person references when the speaker obviously means himself or his audience. In fact, single sentences often jump back and forth between first and third person. It may be that the speakers referred to themselves in the third person, more common in the nineteenth century than it is today. Or it might have been done by recorders who were getting behind in their notes, a standard newspaper trick still used by some "old school" news reporters who don't take shorthand. Since the record presents them as quotes, they are given as such here.

He assured his people he had never been beaten or otherwise abused in prison. To the contrary, he said he had been treated kindly. In turn, he pledged himself to Davis' terms and urged his people to follow suit.

His statement to the delegates concluded, Satanta began speaking to his own people in Kiowa. The interpreter could not understand him, so he was ordered to speak Comanche again, for translation. Instead, he stopped speaking and sat down.

At that point, Lone Wolf apparently grew tired of the speeches, and asked Davis to state his terms. Once the Kiowas heard them, he said they would give an answer.

Davis began by emphasizing that Texas was part of the United States, and the Kiowas and Comanches could no longer view the two as separate powers. Perhaps as much for the federal officials present as the Indians, he pointed out that the U.S. government was required to protect the people of Texas. Despite that, he said the Kiowas and Comanches had been raiding in Texas for years, killing indiscriminately, capturing women and children, and stealing horses. The attacks had been unprovoked. The Texans had not raided into the Indian Territory, but rather had defended their homes. On the other hand, he pointed out that Texas had the power and resources to invade the reservations, as Satanta and Big Tree could attest. But he said the state felt bound to respect the reservations according to the treaty made by the federal government. The Indians, he pointed out, were also bound by treaty, but continually violated it with their raids.

"That thing must now stop, and the Kiowa & Comanche must put themselves in that position that the people of Texas will be satisfied that they canot [sic] go there," the governor said. "I am now going to tell you the terms I demand for Texas. Listen to them."

First, Davis said the Indians were to settle permanently on tillable land on the reservation and begin agriculture. White agents were to remain constantly in their camps and see them all daily. To be doubly sure they could not raid, they were to draw no more than three days' rations. Each man would have to draw rations personally, on a roll call.

Second, he demanded that the Comanches who recently had been raiding into Texas be turned over to state authorities. The Indians who planned to remain friendly were to assist federal troops in hunting down and arresting them. All horses that could be identified as stolen from Texas were to be delivered to their owners, and all captives were to be liberated.

"Satanta and Big Tree will remain in the guard house at Fort Sill, until the commander of the post is satisfied that this arrangement is being carried out in good faith, when he will release them to go with their tribe. But it must be understood by them that they are not to be pardoned, but will be subject to re-arrest and return to the Penitentiary to suffer for their old crime, if at any time the Kiowa violate this arrangement."

Davis concluded by reemphasizing that he had consulted with Smith, Haworth and Davidson, and felt the Indians could comply with the terms if they wanted to. If they did not, he once again pointed out that Texas was ready to go to war to settle the matter permanently.[5]

Satanta's extravagant claims of power and prestige over the plains tribes—claims that Hoag's group apparently accepted at face value—were now being thrown back at him. The governor intended to make him and Big Tree personally responsible for the conduct of the entire Kiowa nation. Smith hurriedly told the Indians that neither he nor the agents had been aware of Davis' terms, and were hearing them for the first time.

---

[5]Ibid., 351-53.

Ironically the threat of force and reprisal was something the Kiowas respected. Unlike the federal officials, these Texans did not beg or bribe. Perhaps, now, the Indians finally were dealing with a man who was their equal. Lone Wolf thought Davis' demands sounded fairly reasonable, and indicated he was ready to agree. He addressed the governor as "my friend" and told him that if Satanta and Big Tree were released, the tribes would accept the terms.

Kicking Bird said delivery of the two chiefs would go a long way toward an understanding. The Comanche Chief Horse Back added his people had made a concerted effort to keep the peace in order to gain the return of Satanta and Big Tree. He acknowledged some of the young warriors had violated the treaty. "But then," he reminded, "the Great Father has not kept all his promises and build [*sic*] houses for them as the agent has promised. Had he done so, we could have kept the young men at home."

To that, Pacer added:

> If the governor can prove that we have stolen horses, we want to be told now, and then we can find out what Indians committed the crime, as we are not all doing it. We do not want our people separated from the whites, but want to live like in Mexico, where we all mix together and be good friends. I do not want to go away from here. I want to be good, but I am afraid of the whites, and dare not come in, and so live wild on the prairie.

At this point, the conference began moving toward other Indian concerns, which the chiefs used to reinforce their positions about Satanta and Big Tree. Quirts Quip, a Yamparika Comanche, said the reservation Indians were being short-changed by the federal government.

"Washington has a lot of money for I saw it in Washington, but I never see any of it here. I do not know what become of it. It must go into the ground."

Thus, he said, Davis' demands were unreasonable.

> The governor is too particular to want all the young men deliv-
> ered up who have raided; they canot [*sic*] be changed in a day & [I]
> don't see why Satanta and Big Tree should still be held, when today
> was looked for, and today they were to be released. You blame us for
> not getting on your road, but you have broken your promises to us
> about houses and farms etc. and you canot blame us for breaking
> some of our promises....I will try to get into the white man's road,
> but it canot be done in a moment. We must have time. Give us
> Satanta and Big Tree and [I] will feel glad and try to do right.

"The Texans have been stealing our horses," the Chief Buffalo Goad said.

"When did the Texans steal your horses," Davis inquired.

"Sometime in July."

"Did you report it to your agents?"

When Buffalo Goad said he had, Davis asked, "How did
you know they were Texans?"

"We have been loosing [sic] them all summer, and did not
know for certain who was doing it; two of my young men five
nights ago found a party running off our horses, and one of
my men was shot by them."

Davis said thefts should be reported to the military authorities immediately. If the thieves escaped into Texas, they
would be extradited back to the Indian Territory for trial and
punishment. He expected justice to work both ways. As for
Satanta and Big Tree, he reiterated that they were state prisoners and that he could have hanged them had he chosen to
do so.

"I will not change the conditions," Davis said. "If they love
Satanta and Big Tree and want them to go to their camps
soon, they must comply with my conditions. And the sooner
they comply, the sooner these chiefs will be released."

Enoch Hoag was desperate. He had gone to the conference

with high hopes that a solution might be reached. Yet Davis sat like an avenging angel, with his catalogue of atrocities against Texas that he was now laying before the federal commissioner. Hoag's prestige was at stake; he was losing face to his Indian charges, and appearing incompetent before his federal superiors. Meanwhile, the governor was unyielding but the Indians did not understand why. Hoag attempted to explain the difference between state and federal authority. He also gave his own assurances that the Kiowas had not been raiding in Texas, based on federal promises of freedom for Satanta and Big Tree.

"Now as their agent, I appeal to His Excellency Davis on behalf of the President and Secretary of the Interior, whether it is not unwise to keep them any longer. I have been instructed by the Dept. to carry out these promises, and they have not the power. All promises their agent made to them came through me from Washington supposing they would be kept," Hoag said.

Davis replied that Hoag had acted on the wrong information.

> Texas has control of this matter entirely, and as to the conditions on which these chiefs should be released, in the conditions I exact, I am governed by a desire to have peace and protect the people of Texas. I think my terms are moderate, and if they desire to comply with them they could do so before many suns. Your agents, Mr Hoag and Mr Hayworth [*sic*], want me to comply with their promises, but I do not agree to their request and will not do so.

Hoag then asked if Davis would leave them at Fort Sill, to be released when Colonel Davidson felt the demands had been met. The governor said he had confidence in Davidson, and felt the Indians could comply within thirty days.

"There is another matter I would like to impress upon the governor, but I don't care about having it interpreted to these

156

Indians, however," Hoag said. "We can place men in their camps who can control them if Satanta & Big Tree is [sic] released, but if they are not...."

"If they are so warlike as that, then we had better settle this matter at once!" Davis interrupted.

Smith saw the situation was getting out of hand. His own patience with Indians and Quakers was wearing very thin. It was becoming obvious that the federal government had been duped by both the Indians and their agents, and that the Indians themselves had been duped by the agents.

"I am now here to demand," the commissioner told the Indians. He reminded them that they had promised to cease raiding if Mackenzie's captives were delivered from Fort Concho. The captives were returned and had hardly settled back into their camps when the young warriors had resumed raiding. "Now I am here to demand those young men of you. And before the sun gets that high tomorrow," he indicated 3 p.m., "I want those men brought here. And when those men are here, you will get your captives and the governor and I will be agreed. Now go home and talk of this, and talk of nothing else."[6]

With that, the conference closed. Now Smith had to make peace with Davis and find a way to extricate the United States from the mess Hoag had created. The federal government considered the Comanches solely responsible for the most recent raids into Texas, and the commissioner intended to have the raiders punished. But the deadline of 3 p.m. the following day came and went and they were not delivered. And Davis was even less bound than before to any promises to release Satanta and Big Tree. This put Smith in a precarious position in his dealings with the Kiowas.

In one last effort, he laid out the problem in writing to

---

[6]Ibid., 353-61.

Davis. He acknowledged that the Kiowas had been promised release of the prisoners "by some misunderstanding" between the state and federal government. On the other hand, he believed the Kiowas had accepted the Indian Bureau's conditions in good faith, and had done their best to adhere to them. They had returned their captives and stolen livestock, and had ceased raiding. In fact, he said they had even gone so far as to restrain the Comanches by killing their ponies and whipping them. He added that even Colonel Davidson was satisfied with their conduct.

On the other hand, Smith told Davis, "Your statement to them yesterday that the chiefs are your prisoners and not in the control of the President while entirely correct cannot be satisfactorily explained to them."

He pointed out that the Indians did not understand the system. They felt that since Satanta and Big Tree were in physical custody of the military, the president of the United States ought to be able to order their release. Because the president did not do so despite federal assurances, the Indians saw a breach of faith. The result was that the Comanches were defying a federal mandate to surrender warriors guilty of raiding, and the Kiowas were too discouraged to bring any pressure on them. Furthermore, the Comanches would be unlikely to surrender the raiders without the use of military force. This would take time and might provoke the Kiowas into joining them in a general uprising. In that case, the commissioner was not at all sure that the government would be in the right.

In view of this, Smith said the government was ready to agree to all of Davis' terms, if only he would free Satanta and Big Tree. They would be strictly on parole, and they or their equals would be turned over to Texas authorities if any more Kiowa raids occurred. There would be a roll call of every male Kiowa aged sixteen and over "with such frequency as to make it impossible for a warrior to be absent from the reservation." The roll would be subject to Davis' inspection. The federal government would make every effort to institute a similar roll call among the Comanches as soon as possible. The government would also use force, if necessary, to compel the Comanches to surrender not less than five raiders "to take the place of Satanta and Big Tree" and would step up patrols along the border with Texas in order the guarantee an end to any further depredations.

Finally came the admission Davis most wanted and the Quakers sought most to avoid:

> Acknowledging fully your control of these prisoners, and disclaiming any responsibility as to the terms of their release, I appeal to the courtesy of the Chief Executive of Texas, to relieve the embarrassment of the Government....

At worst, the release would simply provide the Kiowas with two more fighting men, and Smith doubted they would have much interest in war. On the other hand, he said failure to release them might cause a general war with the Kiowa-Comanche confederation. While there was no doubt of the outcome, it would mean unnecessary loss of life and property along the frontier.[7]

For once, Smith was more correct than he possibly could have imagined. The Kiowas were convinced that Washington had deceived them and that Satanta and Big Tree could be freed only by force. Even Kicking Bird was disillusioned, saying he had "taken the white man by the hand, thinking him to be a friend, but he is not a friend; government has deceived us; Washington is rotten." Lone Wolf decided there was no alternative but fight. He realized this would mean the extinction of the Kiowa people, but he saw no option.[8]

---

[7]Smith to Davis, October 7, 1873, RG 94 4447 AGO 1873.
[8]Battey, *Life and Adventures*, 202-03.

The Kiowas and Comanches met secretly that night, and
made plans to take the prisoners by force. They arrived at the
conference site earlier than the others on Wednesday morning, and quietly positioned warriors with concealed weapons
around the front of the building. Ponies were placed where
Satanta and Big Tree could get to them in a hurry. Some
women were assigned to wander around the edge of the
crowd, so that everything would appear normal. A few Indians struck up conversations with favorite white agency
employees, making vague allusions to death to warn them off.
If Davis held fast, the Indians planned to open fire, killing
him, the small military guard, Smith, the agents and any other
white men who happened to be around.[9]

Davis arrived with Smith's letter in hand. He said it would
not be necessary to translate it to the Indians, but that he
would read it for the benefit of the whites. After finishing that
letter, he read his own reply accepting the government's terms.
Satanta and Big Tree were paroled.

The two prisoners were told to stand. Through Philip
McCusker, Davis told them to make sure the tribes complied
with the terms and ceased raiding. Otherwise, they would be
arrested and returned to prison along with anyone who had
participated in the raids.

"You all now see what a load you have put on my back,"
Smith told the Indians. "The Governor of Texas was going to
keep Satanta and Big Tree until you did what was right and
what he demanded of you. But I promised him that you
should do what was right, and now I want you to promise me
before these Texans and before these other Gentlemen present

---

[9]Ibid.; Nye, *Carbine and Lance*, 174-75. Battey contends that Haworth and Hoag, fully
aware of the Indian plans, defused the situation by "talking with the frontier citizens of Texas,
reasoning with the governor, and pouring oil, as it were, upon the turbulent spirits of the
Indians." The bulk of the evidence, however, indicates Haworth and Hoag had no idea of
what the Kiowas intended, and that the release of Satanta and Big Tree was due solely to the
understanding reached by Smith and Davis.

that you will do what the Governor want[s] you to do." Then he told them to go back to the agency, since he wanted another meeting with them there.[10]

Satanta and Big Tree embraced Davis and the principal chiefs, then mounted horses and followed the Quakers to the agency office. After awhile, Smith arrived with Haworth, McCusker, and various clerks and recorders. The Kiowas and Comanches were represented by virtually all of their principal chiefs. There was not enough room in the office for all the Indians, and those who could not get inside crowded around the windows. Once again, Smith demanded either five Comanches guilty of raiding, or five to serve as hostages in their place. This time, however, he demanded five hostages from the Kiowas as well. That brought an angry outburst, Cartridges slammed into magazines and bowstrings were fitted and tested. When Indians received hostages under these conditions, torture and death were certain. They assumed the whites meant to do the same.

Lone Wolf called for silence. When everyone calmed down, he said the demand was unreasonable and the Indians could not comply. Smith was out of patience and accused Lone Wolf of being childish. This brought another angry outburst. The young warriors listening outside demanded the commissioner's death. The chiefs reprimanded them sharply and they became quiet.

The Comanche Chief Cheevers, whose own band had been living quietly on the reservation for two years, told Smith it was unfair that the peaceful Indians should surrender hostages to cover those who were hostile. He said the raiders could be found west of the Antelope Hills, and the government was welcome to them. But he emphasized that the entire reservation could not be held responsible for the acts of a few.

Smith saw the rationale, and modified his demand. The Indians were given thirty days to round up the raiders. After that,

---

[10]Day and Winfrey, *Texas Indian Papers*, 362-63.

rations would be withheld. Five of Cheevers' Comanches and five Kiowas were furnished to help the troops in the search. They were enrolled as scouts and issued uniforms and weapons.[11]

Davidson had little hope for the success of the venture. In his report, he wrote that Smith's demand for the guilty Indians could only result in a full scale expedition against the Comanches as a whole. The tribe would not give up the raiders without a fight, he said, and recommended the government start timely preparations for a winter campaign.[12]

In Washington, Sherman was just as mystified as the Indians by the events leading to the release of Satanta and Big Tree. It seemed to him that the Government of Texas, which had been crying for relief from Indian raids, had two raiders captured and delivered to it by the army. Then, at the end of two years, these raiders had been turned over to a military detail, conveyed to a military establishment, and placed in the custody of the post commander. Yet the Texas Government insisted it retained jurisdiction. This, in turn, allowed freedom for the two chiefs, whom Sherman would have preferred seeing dead.

Sherman was sick of hearing about Texas and its Indian problems. In his endorsement to Davidson's report, he wrote:

> I suppose General Davidson had no alternative but to accept the trust imposed on him by Governor Davis, but how prisoners in the Guard House at Fort Sill remain in the legal custody of the Governor of Texas passes my understanding. They are subject to the order of the President of the United States. Whatever opinion I may entertain of the wisdom of the parties to this repatriation, I have no doubt that Satanta & Big Tree, in the Guard House at Fort Sill, are subject to the orders of the War Dept.[13]

As Sherman fumed, Cheevers and his "scouts" were leading the detail from Fort Sill on a wild goose chase all over west

---

[11]Nye, *Carbine and Lance*, 175-77.

[12]Davidson to AAG, Department of Texas, October 8, 1873, RG 94 4447 AGO 1873.

[13]Sherman, endorsement to ibid., November 7, 1873. Sherman referred to Davidson by his brevet rank from the Union Army.

Texas. No matter where they went, the raiders managed to stay a jump ahead of the military. Davis offered the use of state troops, but this was rejected by Acting Secretary Cowan.[14] Meanwhile, the Indians raided into Texas again, striking in Wichita and Palo Pinto Counties. One veteran of the Sioux campaigns of 1858 and 1859 wrote the governor that "judging from previous Experience I firmly believe the only effectual method of forever disposing [sic] of this Indian question is to organize a force sufficiently strong to push into the heart of their territory and teach them a lesson that will be remembered for the next twenty five years at least." Another man wrote, "It's evident they do not intend to comply with their agreement and will continue to come in and depredate on us until they are thoroughly whipped and made to know they have to stay away."[15]

The Texans themselves were in an uproar over the release of Satanta and Big Tree. Davis was vilified in newspapers throughout the state, and petitions called for his impeachment. In the midst of this, Sherman was summoned before a congressional committee on military affairs to explain the situation. He testified grudgingly, making no voluntary statements, answering only those questions that were asked. He told the committee why he went to Texas, of Satanta's boasts of the raid, of the arrest and the reasons why he sent the chiefs back to Texas for trial. As before, he indicated Satanta, at least, should have been executed, and that Davis had been remiss in commuting the sentence.

Davis took exception to Sherman's statements, which he considered thoughtless. He suggested that Sherman should have taken the responsibility for any executions, because the chiefs were arrested under military jurisdiction. Likewise, he said they

---

[14]Nye, *Carbine and Lance,* 177-79; Cowan to Davis, October 18, 1873, Day and Winfrey, *Texas Indian Papers,* 363.

[15]"judging from previous experience…" F.A. Blake to Davis, October 23, 1873; "It's evident they do not intend…" E.B. Baines to Davis, October 30, 1873, both in Day and Winfrey, *Texas Indian Papers,* 364-66.

were guilty of acts of "savage warfare," rather than civil crimes against the state, and this, again, came under military law. Davis also felt betrayed both by the military and the Indian Bureau because no satisfactory effort had been made to round up the raiders or hostages and, in fact, raids into Texas were on the rise.

This was too much for Sherman. He wrote Davis that far from issuing thoughtless statements, he had "thought of the subject a hundred times...."

As for jurisdiction, he said:

> You are in error in supposing that I had any authority whatever to execute them at Fort Sill; or to order their trial by a Military Court or Commission. I had authority to do exactly what I did, viz: with the assent and approval of the Agent, Tatum on the spot, to send them to the jurisdiction of the Court having authority to try and punish. Once there they passed under a Texas Court, and under your authority as the Governor of the State. Without the interposition of your authority, these murderers could have been hung as a matter of course, but you remitted them to the Penitentiary, and then afterwards set them free.

> I believe in making the tour of your frontier with a small escort, I ran the risk of my life, and I said to the Military Committee what I now say to you, that I will not again voluntarily assume that risk in the interest of your Frontier, that I believe Satanta and Big Tree will have their revenge, if they have not already had it, and that *if they are to have scalps that yours is the first that should be taken* [italics added].

> I can make all allowances to the kind gentlemen of Philadelphia, who were so busy in accomplishing the release of these two murderers but I was amazed that you, who felt the constant inflictions of these Texas Raids should have yielded. As to the promises made you at Fort Sill at the time of releasing of Satanta and Big Tree, I know nothing at all, and leave the Civil Agents of the Govt. to reconcile their actions with these promises as best they can.[16]

With that, Sherman washed his hands of the whole affair. In his view, he had done his part as best he could. Davis was now on his own.

---

[16]Sherman to Davis, February 17, 1874, Sherman, Unofficial Correspondence.

Part 6: The Aftermath

CHAPTER 12

"I am Tired of Fighting and Do Not Want to Fight Anymore"

Sherman was correct in his assumption that the raids would continue, but he may have been wrong in saying Satanta would be involved. The long ordeal of his arrest, trial and imprisonment had made the old chief realistic about whites and their power. He had seen Texans first hand and understood them better than he ever had before. They were a different breed from the people sent from Washington. While the federal government could be manipulated, he knew Davis had been deadly serious in saying that he would be returned to prison if there was any trouble. The fight had left him. As long as he was free to roam his plains, he would remain quiet.

Shortly after his release, he stood talking with some other chiefs just outside of Fort Sill. He picked up and handful of sand and let it fall through is fingers to the ground.

"The white men are as numerous as the sands in these hills," he remarked. Then he pointed to some soldiers loitering about the post and added, "We may kill these, but others will come. The Indians' days are over."[1]

Lone Wolf shared that opinion, but planned to continue raiding anyway. For him, it had become a personal matter. In December 1873, a war party including his favorite son and a

---

[1]Wharton, *Satanta*, 238.

fifteen-year-old nephew had raided across Texas and into
Coahuila. As it headed home, it was attacked at Kickapoo
Springs in south Texas, by a unit of Fourth Cavalry under
Lieutenant Charles L. Hudson. Among the dead were Lone
Wolf's son and nephew. When the news reached the Indian
Territory the following month, Lone Wolf cut off his hair,
killed his horses and burned his possessions in sign of deep
mourning. Now, like old Satank before him, he lived only for
revenge. He bided his time and waited for the appropriate
moment.[2]

Throughout the winter and spring of 1874, the plains sim-
mered. Heavy rains disrupted freight service bringing government supplies. Haworth had to put the Indians on half rations
and they went hungry. It was the raiding season again, and the
restless young warriors began killing cattle at random. Finally,
Haworth had to reactivate Tatum's military police program.[3]

About the same time, Satanta ran into C.F. Doan, who
operated a store near Fort Sill. Doan liked the Indians, and
often gave candy and crackers to the women and children.
This made him popular even with the Kiowa war faction.
Now Satanta gave him a warning. The Indians planned to rise
and kill every white in the territory. They wanted Doan and
his family to leave before trouble started.[4]

It is unlikely Satanta himself planned to be involved in any
trouble, but he no doubt would have known if something was
brewing. Whatever his intentions and regardless of his overall
good behavior, Satanta remained suspect. He had taken to fol-

---

[2]Hudson to Post Adjutant, Fort Clark, Texas, December 15, 1873, in "Official Correspondence," *Museum Journal,* 10:67-69; Nye, *Carbine and Lance,* 182-84.

[3]Richardson, "Comanche Indians," 4:26.

[4]Doan, "Reminiscences," 775. Doan says Satanta's warning came before he attacked a
wagon train, indicating the Warren massacre. However, that was in 1871, and Doan did not
come to the area until 1874. He seems to have confused the Warren raid with the outbreak of
the Red River War, understandable when one considers that he was writing fifty years later,
and there is no real evidence Satanta attacked any trains after his release from prison.

lowing black soldiers who were returning to Fort Sill from the post trader's store, a violation of a general order that prohibited Indians from entering the post proper. One night in May 1874, he followed a trooper to the stables, where a sentry challenged him and told him he was under arrest. He backed away, then yelled, "Kicking Bird!" and turned and ran toward the Kiowa camps. He shouted that the soldiers were coming to attack them and ordered them to pack and prepare to move.

Fortunately, Kicking Bird and several others were asleep in the trader's store. When some of the young warriors came to tell them what was going on, they sent word back to settle down.

With any other Indian, it would have been shrugged off as a minor incident. But this was Satanta, and the post commander, Captain C.A. Carlton, was immediately suspicious.

"I think he considered himself liable to arrest and thought if he could induce his people to run away from the Post and make them afraid to return[,] he might regain his influence and give us trouble," Carlton told Haworth the following day. "He gives a variety of reasons for the affair this morning."[5]

On the reservation, the surveys continued and the roll calls commenced, adding to the resentment among the superstitious Kiowas. But there was a new factor involved that threatened the very existence of life as the plains tribes knew it. Early in the decade, a process had been developed to turn buffalo skins into high quality industrial leather. This created an entirely new industry. Three or four months on the plains with a .50-caliber Sharps rifle might yield a man as much as $2,000, a small fortune in the nineteenth century. Hunts became highly organized, with massive support systems, and Dodge City, Kansas, became the center of the hide trade. With methodical precision, the hunters swept down through

---

[5]Carlton to Haworth, May 8, 1874, Kiowa File.

the plains, slaughtering buffalo by the tens of thousands. Soon, the northern herds were gone, and they turned their attention toward the southern herds.

The Indians panicked. The buffalo was the linchpin of their economy. It provided meat for food, skins for clothing and lodges, and by-products for anything else they might need. When all other resources, such as government rations, failed they could still hunt the buffalo. In fact, the animal itself had become a totemic figure, and the annual hunt had taken on a near religious significance.[6]

Now something unusual happened. In desperation the normally secular Comanches raised a prophet and medicine man of their own. His name was Isa-tai, and he gained prestige as a seer whose predictions invariably were correct. By the spring of 1874, he was a powerful figure. He convinced many that he could make them bullet-proof, and that he could vomit cartridges from his stomach by the thousands. Isa-tai had lost an uncle in the Kickapoo Springs fight and, like Lone Wolf, burned for revenge. Among his followers was Quahadi Chief Quanah Parker, by now one of the most important Comanche warlords.

In May, Isa-tai took the unprecedented step of calling the Comanches together for a Sun Dance. One old chief warned Haworth, who was more amused than concerned. But when the agent sent a peace feeler to the Quahadis, they notified him to stay out of the way if he valued his life. On May 13, the Comanche bands came for their rations. They were docile, but plans for the dance continued. When it finally convened, the chiefs held a council and decided to go to war. Delegations were sent to summon the Kiowas, Arapahos and Cheyennes. Most of the Arapahos ignored the summons, but a small delegation of disaffected warriors came. The principal chiefs of

---

[6]For an analysis of the buffalo's influence on Indian development and destruction, see Robinson, *The Buffalo Hunters*.

the Cheyennes moved their camps in close to the agency at Darlington, but the Dog Soldier faction opted for war and commanded a substantial following. The Kiowas were divided. Since they had not yet held their Sun Dance, only the most incorrigible war chiefs went to the Comanche gathering.[7]

Initially, the Comanches had planned to settle scores with their old enemies, the Tonkawas, at Fort Griffin. But word reached the commanding officer at Griffin that something was up, and he moved them onto the post. Instead, the hostiles decided to destroy a hide trading center that had sprung up near Adobe Walls in the Texas Panhandle, and make an example by massacring the hunters there.

The attack began at dawn, June 27. Isa-tai spurred the Indians on, assuring them that his medicine would make them safe. But they could not withstand the superb marksmanship and high-powered rifles of the buffalo hunters. Though vastly outnumbered, the defenders kept up a steady, punishing fire until the Indians pulled back. After that, the warriors settled behind cover, and the battle wound down to sniping between the lines. The hunters heard a bugler among the Indians, and those who had served in the army recognized the calls and noticed the Indians were maneuvering to them. The story has since arisen that it was Satanta, but Billy Dixon, who was in the fight, made no mention of him by name. Instead, he felt it was a Mexican captive who had been adopted into the tribe. Besides, Thomas Battey had seen Satanta around the agency during the time of the Adobe Walls fight.[8]

Eventually, the Indians gave up the fight, and their failure to destroy Adobe Walls ruined Isa-tai's prestige. But the

---

[7]Haley, *Buffalo War*, 52-58. The Cheyenne Agency near Camp Supply had been renamed Darlington, following the death of Agent Brinton Darlington on May 1, 1872 (See Butler, "Pioneer School Teaching," 526n).

[8]Dixon, *"Billy" Dixon*, 163; Wharton, *Satanta*, 227.

uprising, now begun, had to follow its course; the Indians were too frustrated to let it die. Many Cheyennes and Arapahos went over to the hostile side, and Captain Carlton suspected that Lone Wolf had taken a party of Kiowas to Texas. He had, but he was not the leader, and the strike itself was only a preliminary.

At Darlington, Agent Miles broke Quaker tradition and called for troops to protect the white personnel. They were dispatched from Fort Sill, but diverted to protect Richards' Wichita Agency at Anadarko in Sill's immediate jurisdiction. Troops from Kansas were sent to cover Darlington. The Quaker Policy was finished.[9]

South of the Red River there were also changes affecting the military situation. Edmund Davis had been soundly defeated at the polls in December 1873, and Democrat Richard Coke was elected governor. The Democratic Party took every state-wide office, and dominated the legislature and local positions. After exhausting legal means to void the election, Davis called out a company of black militia to keep him in office, and cabled Washington for assistance. When Grant refused to intervene, Davis called out a second company of militia, the Travis Rifles. But the Rifles mutinied and declared for the new government, and when Grant once again refused to intervene, Davis knew it was over.[10] Coke and the Democrats took office and one the first acts of the Democratic legislature was to authorize a new battalion of Rangers for frontier defense. It would operate wherever it was needed, independently of the army. The Texans were declaring their intention to fight back.

Now it was the Kiowas' turn for their Sun Dance. In their slow, deliberate way they argued and debated, much to the

---

[9]Carlton to Haworth, May 8, 1874, Kiowa File; Mooney, *Calendar History*, 338; Nye, *Carbine and Lance*, 191-92.

[10]Ramsdell, *Reconstruction*, 314-17.

frustration of the Comanches. Kicking Bird spoke for the peace faction, while Lone Wolf argued for war. One by one the chiefs threw in with Kicking Bird. Finally, the paramount medicine man, Nap-a-wat, cast his lot with the peace party, and the war faction collapsed. Individual Kiowas might put together raiding parties, but the Kiowa nation would not support them.

The time came for Satanta to declare his position. With some ceremony, he gave his medicine lance—one of two in the tribe—to A'to-t'aiñ, another renown warrior. His heirloom medicine shield went to his son, Tsa'l-au-te. This was final. It meant he had voluntarily abdicated his position as a principal chief, and would never again go to war. When the Sun Dance ended, Kicking Bird led three-fourths of the Kiowa nation to enroll as neutrals at Fort Sill. Satanta's band went its own way. Lone Wolf was free to gather support where he could—if he could.[11]

Once again, the Do-ha-te Maman-ti emerged from the shadows. He was as widely respected and personally popular as ever, and on July 10, he told the war faction that he would lead the long-awaited vengeance raid for Lone Wolf's son and nephew. The renegades took new heart and began celebrating. Battle songs rang through the hills, and women and young girls danced around the medicine lodge. The entire camp was summoned to the do-ha-te's lodge after dark. They sat and waited, and soon heard the familiar rustle of wings and the cry of the owl. Maman-ti came out.

"The revenge raid will be a success," he said. "At least one enemy will be killed. None of us will die."

The camp rushed to make ready and at midnight Maman-

---

[11]Haley, *Buffalo War*, 79-81; Wharton, *Satanta*, 220. Wharton says Satanta gave his medicine shield to A'to-t'aiñ as part of the gift of the lance, but the Kiowas say it went to Tsa'l-au-te. The shield is now in the Phoebe Hearst Museum of the University of California at Berkeley, a gift of General Hugh Scott who the Kiowa say illegally obtained it from Tsa'l-au-te.

ti and Lone Wolf led about fifty warriors toward the Red River and Texas. On the morning of July 12, the party came out onto the Salt Creek Prairie. To the east, the wagon road from Jacksboro to Fort Griffin came around Cox Mountain and out onto the plains.

"This is the place where we killed the wagon teamsters!" one Indian shouted, and suggested they visited the grave of Or-dlee, the Comanche killed during the Warren massacre. They rode over to the spot on the hill where they had hidden the body and examined the weathered pile of bones. Then they descended the hill, rode across the prairie and up to the top of Cox Mountain. They ate and rested, but the loneliness of the place made the superstitious Kiowas nervous.

Suddenly one of them spotted four cowboys. They came down the hill and charged across the prairie. But they had been riding hard since they left home, and their ponies were exhausted and had bleeding feet. Maman-ti saw no chance to catch up with the cowboys, who were riding away as fast as their horses could take them. He pointed to some cattle grazing nearby, and ordered several killed the make rawhide shoes for the ponies, while the mounts themselves were allowed to rest. When that was done, they rode over to some low hills to scout the valley beyond. Again the warriors became nervous, but Lone Wolf reminded them of their goal—to kill Texans.

About that time, someone noticed a large group of Texans coming toward them. As the Indians watched, it became obvious the Texans had seen them as well. They were heavily armed and ready to fight. Maman-ti decided that he and another warrior should ride down into the valley as decoys and drawn the Texans toward the others.

The Texans were a company of the new Frontier Battalion commanded by Major John B. Jones. They had struck the trail of this same group of Indians and had been following it for several hours. Maman-ti's plan worked, and the Rangers were completely surprised. Fortunately, Jones remained calm and kept them organized. The men managed to find cover and both sides settled down for a siege. As the Rangers grew low on water, Mel Porter and Dave Bailey disobeyed orders and made for a nearby water hole with several canteens. A large group of Indians came down on them. Porter escaped back to his own lines, but Bailey was overwhelmed. Lone Wolf personally chopped his head to pieces and cut out his bowels. Then the entire group mutilated the body. The first coup had been counted by the warrior Mamaday-te, a friend of Lone Wolf's dead son. The grateful father now had his revenge and bestowed his own name on Mamaday-te, who became Young Lone Wolf.

With the day drawing to a close, the Kiowas held a brief victory celebration and started home, while Jones' battered command made its way to a nearby ranch, then back to Fort Richardson. In addition to Bailey, a second Ranger had died of wounds during the afternoon. Not a single Indian had been lost. Once again, Maman-ti's prophecies were correct.

Incredibly, the raiders were met at the Red River by a summons from Haworth, sent through Kicking Bird, to return to the agency immediately. Hoag had ordered the agent to round up all Indians under his care, so that the military would not attack them on the plains. They were literally smuggled into the agency and placed under its protection, although there could be no doubt that they had been out raiding.[12] Once humanitarians, Hoag and Haworth had become accessories to common murder.

---

[12]Nye, *Carbine and Lance*, 192-200. The action is known at the Lost Valley Fight. Like the Indian version of the Warren massacre, anyone attempting to reconstruct the Kiowa side must rely on Nye, who heard it first hand from participants or members of their immediate families. He also visited some of the sites with Hunting Horse, a member of the raiding party. There are numerous accounts of Jones' side, including his own reports in the Adjutant General's files in the State Archive in Austin. For a recent evaluation of Jones' role in the fight, see Robinson, "The Tough Little Ranger of Lost Valley," 18-22.

PART 6:   THE AFTERMATH

Lone Wolf's raid was but one more preliminary to the much larger rising. As the majority of the Kiowas huddled around Fort Sill and Satanta's band minded its own business out on the plains, the Comanches, Southern Cheyennes, and disaffected Kiowas and Arapahos were consolidating and organizing. As General Augur noted in his annual report:

> The line between the friendly and hostile bands is now well defined and if the Government will persevere in its present attitude, the latter will soon be forced into such entire submission as shall secure peace to our borders for many years.[13]

The federal government fully intended to persevere. There was no more talk of peace or annuities or appeasement. The Quakers had been given their chance; it had led to unending slaughter on the plains and, ultimately, to a major rebellion. Grimly the generals marshalled their forces in the states and territories surrounding the Southern Plains. Attacking forces were organized. Zones of operation and command were assigned. The final link was now forged in the chain of events that had begun three years before with the Warren Wagon Train Massacre—the United States went to war.

Although raids extended into Kansas, most of the action occurred in the Red River area and, for that reason, the rising is known to history as the Red River War. The government's plan was simple—a four-pronged offensive consisting of Colonel Nelson A. Miles, Fifth Infantry, moving south from Fort Dodge, Kansas; Davidson west from Fort Sill; Major William R. Price, Eighth Infantry, east from Fort Bascom, New Mexico; and Mackenzie, reinforced by Lieutenant Colonel George Buell's forces, north from the headwaters of the Brazos River in Texas. The plan was to compress the Indians into a small area and subdue them. Instructing his departmental commanders, General Sheridan wrote:

---

[13]Augur, Annual Report, September 28, 1874, "Official Correspondence," *Museum Journal,* 10:108-109.

In conducting operations against the Indians—either for the purpose of punishing them, or the protection of persons and property against their depredations—the Commanding Officers [of the] Departments of the Missouri and Texas may disregard the line separating those departments.[14]

General Augur expanded on those instructions by telling Mackenzie:

The object of the proposed Campaign against the hostile Cheyennes, Comanches, Kiowas, and others from the Fort Sill Reservation is to punish them for recent depredations along the Kansas and Texas frontiers, and you are expected to take such measures against them as will, in your judgment, the soonest accomplish the purpose.[15]

Throughout the late summer and fall, the soldiers swept the plains. Colonel Miles pressed the Indians from the east along the Red River, while Price came down the Canadian, forcing them into the Staked Plains of Texas where Mackenzie was moving into position.[16] The decisive battle was fought in Palo Duro Canyon on September 28, 1874, when Mackenzie destroyed a major encampment of Comanches, Kiowas and Cheyennes. The leader of the Kiowas was Maman-ti, who had assured them they would be safe in the canyon.[17]

Maman-ti and many others escaped during the attack, but Mackenzie had thrown them back against Miles and Davidson. With their camp, ponies and stores destroyed by Mackenzie, they could only hope, at best, to avoid the soldiers as long as possible. For the Indians, it was no longer a question of raiding—it now was merely survival. Yet during these weeks, one question often must have come up in the minds of many army officers—Where was Satanta?

He and Big Tree had registered on August 6 at Fort Sill,

[14]General Order No. 4, MilDivMo, July 10, 1874, ibid., 77-78.
[15]Augur to Mackenzie, August 28, 1874, ibid., 80.
[16]Sheridan to Sherman, September 5, 1874, ibid., 90-91.
[17]Ibid., 122n-23n.

where they received certificates saying they were not to be bothered "unless engaged in acts of hostility or away from camp without permission." Satanta himself acknowledged being away from camp and at the Wichita Agency on August 22, when a fight broke out between Davidson's troops and Comanches supported by Kiowas. After striking back out onto the plains, he and Big Tree showed up at Darlington in early October. This time Satanta was ready to surrender. His band consisted of 145 men, women and children in twenty-four lodges. He also had thirteen rifles, three pistols, eighteen bows and four lances, which he turned over to Lieutenant Thomas Neill of the Sixth Cavalry, whose troops were guarding the agency.

"I am tired of fighting and do not want to fight any more," Satanta said. "I came in here to give myself up and do as the white chief wishes. I want to cultivate a farm at the Cheyenne Agency here. I do not like the Agency at Fort Sill. I am half Arapahoe [sic], half Kiowa, and I want to live near the Arapahos. At Fort Sill the Comanches would go on the war path, and raid in Texas, whilst the Kiowas would be blamed for their bad acts. I have done no fighting against the whites, have killed no white men and committed no depredations since I left Fort Sill.

"When the fight commenced at the Wichita Agency, all were excited, I packed up and left, and took no part in the fight. Soon after, I left the Kiowas and Comanches, who have gone to the Staked Plains, and I remained at [the] headwaters of the Washita with the party now with me."

It was a good speech, and in some ways was strangely prophetic of the one Chief Joseph would later deliver when he surrendered the Nez Perces. It availed Satanta little. He and Big Tree were placed under close guard as hostages, and the rest of the band was interned.[18]

---

[18]Neill to AAG, Department of the Missouri, October 4, 1874, ibid., 125-26.

CHAPTER 12: "I AM TIRED OF FIGHTING"

The extent of Satanta's involvement in the war cannot be certain. He has been accused of joining the hostiles and participating in raids and fighting. By his own admission, he was present when some fighting occurred, and may have been a spectator. That in itself was enough. His boasting from prison that he controlled the plains tribes and would guarantee their conduct, the actual parole that guaranteed an end to all raids by Kiowas, and his mere presence when fighting occurred—all were sufficient grounds to send him back to prison. Big Tree was allowed to remain under arrest at Fort Sill. To the generals, he was small fish. They wanted Satanta.

On November 5, the old chief, chained and under guard, left Fort Sill for Huntsville. Twelve days later, Governor Coke notified Captain Carlton that Satanta "has been received and properly lodged in the penitentiary."[19] He would never see the plains again.

---

[19]Carlton to Coke, November 3, 1874, and endorsement/reply, November 17, 1874, Day and Winfrey, *Texas Indian Papers*, 366 (erroneously listed as "C.H. Carlton to E.J. Davis"; Davis was no longer governor).

CHAPTER 13
"There is Some Confusion As to Names"

The Red River War officially ended with the surrender of Quanah Parker on June 2, 1875. But for most of the Indians it was finished by mid-April. By then, the bulk of the resistance had collapsed and many prime movers of the rebellion were prisoners at Fort Sill. Lone Wolf and Maman-ti surrendered on February 26,[1] to be joined later by White Horse and Eagle Heart. Thus, after almost four years, all the leaders of the Warren Wagon Train Massacre were either dead or in custody.

The government decided to send the most incorrigible chiefs to Fort Marion, Florida, for internment. Kicking Bird was assigned the unenviable task of designating who would go. He refused. While he had often opposed the war party, he would not betray his own people. But Colonel Davidson played the Kiowa political factions against each other, and in the end, Kicking Bird made the selections. Lone Wolf, Maman-ti and White Horse were among those chosen. The bulk of the slots, however, Kicking Bird managed to fill with obscure young warriors, unpopular tribesmen, general troublemakers, and Mexican captives. In all, more than thirty Kiowas were named for transportation to Florida from Fort Sill alone, compared to only nine Comanches. This infuriated the Kiowas because most of the tribe had been neutral during

[1]Haley, *Buffalo War*, 205, 209.

the war. But the government was inflexible and the ratio remained unchanged.[2]

The Kiowa prisoners, fully aware of Maman-ti's power, began pressuring the do-ha-te to put a death spell on Kicking Bird. On April 28, as they were loaded into wagons for the first leg of their journey to the ancient cells of Fort Marion, Kicking Bird rode up.

"Brothers," he said, "the time has come to say good-bye. I am sorry for you. But because of your stubbornness, I have failed to keep you out of trouble. You will have to be punished by the government. Take your medicine. It will not be for long. I love you and will work for your release. I have done my best to keep you in the right road, and I hope that the time will come soon when you will return to us happy, at peace and of a different mind."

Maman-ti glared at him.

"You think you have done well, Kicking Bird. You remain free, a big man with the whites. But you will not live long."

The wagons pulled out.

On May 4, Kicking Bird went into convulsions shortly after drinking his morning coffee. Haworth was summoned, and sent for the agency physician. By mid-morning, however, Kicking Bird knew he was dying.

"I have taken the white man's road," he told Haworth. "I am not sorry for it. Tell my people to keep in the good path."[3] Although Kicking Bird had never accepted Christianity, Haworth took it upon himself to give the chief a Christian burial.

Lawrie Tatum, who probably knew Kicking Bird as well as anyone, wrote:

---

[2]Pratt, *Battlefield and Classroom*, 91-94, 105-06. Fort Marion is better known by its Spanish name of Castillo de San Marcos, and was about two hundred years old when the Indians arrived there.

[3]Nye, *Carbine and Lance*, 233.

Although he was only in middle life he was the leading chief of the Kiowa Indians, and for at least six years previous to his death his influence was always on the side of right. He lived to see the hostile element of his tribe brought into subjection, and all of the Indians in the Indian Territory on friendly terms with the Government....[4]

The post surgeon at Fort Sill attributed the death to poison, probably in Kicking Bird's coffee, and speculated it was a vendetta within the tribe. The Kiowas knew better. Maman-ti had prayed him to death. But in doing so, the do-ha-te had violated the laws of his medicine and invited a terrible retribution upon himself. He developed consumption, failed rapidly, and died at Fort Marion on July 29, 1875.[5]

One by one, the main characters of the Warren Wagon Train Massacre and subsequent Kiowa raids eased out of the scene. Satanta was completely broken now. He idled about the prison, sometimes making bows and arrows, but generally sprawling aimlessly on his familiar pile of oakum in the workshop, alone with his thoughts. He never bothered anyone, and prison officially generally left him to himself. Often he could be seen staring northward toward the Red River and home.

As time passed and his health began to fail, he became a sympathetic figure. On August 10, 1878, Thomas J. Goree, superintendent of the penitentiary, wrote the agent at Fort Sill, "Satanta is here, in declining health, and very feeble. If he remains here [he] can not live long. Will heartily second any effort made for his release."[6]

No effort was made. The sixty-one-year-old Satanta was now more of a symbol than a man, and the government was determined that symbol would remain behind bars. On October 10, W.A. Morris and Joe Bryant of Montague County

---

[4]Tatum, *Red Brothers*, 197.

[5]Nye, *Carbine and Lance*, 234; Pratt, *Battlefield and Classroom*, 143.

[6]Nye, *Carbine and Lance*, 244; Wharton, *Satanta*, 234; Thomas J. Goree to P. B. Hunt, August 10, 1878, Kiowa File.

stopped by to see him. Satanta asked Morris if he thought the government might ever release him. On being told it was unlikely, he became despondent.

"I cannot wither and die like a dog in chains," he said.[7]

The following morning, the old chief slashed his wrists. He was taken to the prison hospital where, left unattended, he jumped from a second story landing, smashing his head on the pavement below. He was buried in a potter's field known as Peckerwood Hill that the prison still uses for a cemetery.

Two months later, a mysterious woman went to the marble yard of Thomas E. Byrne in Houston. She was heavily veiled and refused to give her name. She ordered a monument inscribed *Satanta, Chief of the Kiowas,* to be delivered to the grave on Peckerwood Hill, and paid $127 in cash. The monument was placed over the grave but later disappeared.[8]

By the time of Satanta's death, the Kiowa-Comanche Agency was run by P. B. Hunt, an Episcopalian who replaced the ailing Haworth on April 1, 1878. A month later the surviving Florida prisoners were allowed to return to the reservation. Among them was Lone Wolf, who died the following year during a malaria outbreak on the reservation. The agency itself was relocated to the north, across the Washita River from Anadarko. The Indians had been doing well, and some of the young raiders even changed sides, enlisting in the army as scouts. The government felt it was time to show confidence by moving the agency away from the military at Fort Sill.[9]

Lawrie Tatum returned to farming in Iowa after his resignation. Although he felt his mission was a failure, in retrospect he may have been the greatest of agents. His blend of toughness and compassion postponed open warfare and gave the government time to permanently win over important

---

[7]"Indian Brave Back at Home," Dallas *Time-Herald,* June 30, 1963.

[8]Huckabay, *Ninety-four Years,* 202; Tolbert, "Remains of Chief Satanta Moved from Prison Grave," Dallas *News,* June 26, 1963; Texas Prison Papers.

[9]Tatum, *Red Brothers,* 202; Nye, *Carbine and Lance,* 254.

leaders like Kicking Bird. When war finally came, the large number of neutral chiefs made it much less bloody than it might have been.

Fate was less kind to Ranald Mackenzie. He served in the field until 1882, when he was promoted to brigadier general. In December 1883, shortly after becoming commander of the Department of Texas, he suffered a mental breakdown and three months later was retired from the army. He died in New York in 1889.

Samuel Lanham's prosecution of Satanta and Big Tree propelled him to fame. He served ten years in the federal congress, and was elected governor in 1902. He retired at the end of a successful two-year term, and died in Weatherford on July 29, 1908.[10]

Of all the chiefs who lived through the stormy collapse of Kiowa military might, Big Tree adapted most readily to the white man's road. As the furor over the Red River War died down, he was allowed to go his own way. A new day was dawning for the Kiowas, and it would profoundly affect his life. One of the first indications was a letter that Captain J. L. Hall received at Fort Sill from Joshua Givens, a Kiowa university student in Pennsylvania, in November 1885.

> This is my last year in the College here, and will probably return to your Agency next summer. And if I do, I will come back to East again in the fall. My intention is to study Theology and then go out into the broad world for battle....
>
> I am the son of old Satanka, who was killed at Fort Sill, for being refused to go to the Texans Penitentiary....Big Tree and Satanta were taken and came back again in two years.[11]

---

[10]Texans generally view the governorship as more prestigious than the U.S. House or Senate. Governors are generally older people who are elected after distinguished service on the state or federal level. With the notable exceptions of W. Lee O'Daniel, who moved from the governorship to the U.S. Senate in 1941, and John Connally, who could have virtually anything he wanted, outgoing governors are expected to retire gracefully, and historically those who try to parlay the office into a federal position do so at their political peril.

[11]Givens to Hall, November 21, 1885, Kiowa File.

Joshua L. Givens, whose father had been considered the worst of the Kiowas, completed his seminary studies and returned to the Indian Territory as a Presbyterian missionary. His sister, Splice-Hair, who took the name Julia Givens, also was educated in the east, and likewise returned as a missionary.[12]

For some time, Big Tree had been interested in the white man's theology and, remembering his old association with Satank, took the young Kiowa minister under wing and assisted whenever he could. A crisis came in 1887, when a new prophet arose. His name was P'oinkia and, like Isa-tai of the Comanches, he claimed he could make the Kiowas bullet-proof. He told them they must abandon every aspect of white life and return to primitive ways. He further insisted that all food be blessed by him and a special ceremony be used for eating. Thus they could defeat the whites and reclaim their country. The Kiowas were ready for anything, and P'oinkia attracted a large following.

Refusing to be bluffed, Big Tree and several of his friends openly defied P'oinkia's edicts and the prophet began to lose face. Still, he had the potential of being a powerful adversary and three troops of cavalry were sent to Anadarko in case of trouble. Joshua Givens received permission to try his luck with P'oinkia. Meeting the medicine man, he disputed his position. P'oinkia replied he would rule all the Kiowas except for the Big Tree faction, which would be killed by a cyclone.

Joshua then issued a challenge. Two army officers would shoot P'oinkia through the heart. If, on the third day, he arose again from the dead, all would know he was the true Messiah. The prophet declined and his influence faded.

No longer bothered by P'oinkia, Big Tree continued leaning toward white religion and eventually headed a delegation that asked for a Baptist mission at Rainey Mountain. He joined

---

[12]Huckabay, *Ninety-four Years*, 203.

the church in 1897 and became a deacon. From time to time, he would witness to the Lord's power of forgiveness, recalling a raid in Montague County when he had smashed the head of a baby with his pistol and thrown it at the feet of its mother. He always ended the story by saying, "God has forgiven me, and I did that hideous thing."

In 1903, when he was past fifty, he risked his life in a flash flood to save the life of a white man. Ironically the white was an Indian hater and did not even bother to thank him.

When Big Tree died on November 13, 1929, he was a leader among his people, respected by Indian and white alike.[13]

In retrospect, the Warren Wagon Train Massacre was a turning point in post-Civil War affairs on the Southern Plains. It attracted national attention to the war-torn Texas frontier. It ended thirty-five years of military indifference and filled the generals with a single-minded resolve. It gave Tatum the time he needed to win the peace chiefs. And it set off the chain of events that resulted in the final conquest of the area.

Yet the raid and its impact were lost in the broad sweep of action during the last twenty years of the Indian Wars. It had occurred early in that period. And as the government overwhelmed Sioux, Northern Cheyenne, Nez Perce and Western Apache, it came to be viewed almost as a local problem. No where is this more clearly seen than in an interdepartmental memo in Washington in January 1887.

> Brig Gen. R.C. Drum USA
> Adjutant General
> War Department
>
> General:
> The bearer of this note is a Kiowa, Joshua Given [sic], who desires to obtain the exact date of the death of his father and the circumstances attending it.

---

[13]Ibid., 203-06; Nye, *Carbine and Lance* 268-70; Morris, "Big Tree's Raid," 1-3.

From the records of this Office it would seem that he was shot while under arrest, near Ft. Sill, in June, 1871; but as he was at that time in the charge of the military, and there is some confusion as to names, he desires to know the War Department Record on the matter. He gives the name of his father as Satanka while in the account of what seems to be his capture and death he is referred to as Satanta.

I shall be glad if you can put him in the way of obtaining the accurate information which he desires.

> Yours respectfully
> J.D.C. Atkins
> Commissioner[14]

After less than sixteen years, the facts seemed to have slipped away.

---

[14]Atkins to Drum, January 7, 1887, Letters Received.

Epilogue

The principal Kiowas of the Warren Wagon Train Massacre represented three generations, each with its own relationship to the whites.

Satank, born near the end of the eighteenth century, was a Kiowa of the plains, uninfluenced by the outside world. Proud and defiant, he was a warrior to the end, first in his effort to stab Colonel Grierson at Fort Sill, then with his suicidal attack on the guards.

Big Tree was the youngest, born and reared in a world that was already becoming white. Respecting, perhaps even admiring the technological and demographic superiority of the whites, he quickly realized that his survival depended on accommodating them. This he did, first by restraining Satank from killing Grierson, then by his conduct in prison, and finally by embracing and promoting the white religion.

Satanta was in a category all his own. Even his most ardent supporters must admit that he was a cold-blooded killer. But if he is to be judged, he must be judged by the society in which he lived. It was a treaty society—neither Kiowa nor white, but a perversion of both. The raid into Texas was an effort to be a real Kiowa.

His conduct during his arrest and trial led men to call him a woman and a coward. He continually changed his story, made false promises, and tried to shift the blame to others. The whites took this to mean he was afraid of death. The Kiowas knew better. Satanta was never afraid to die, but he would use any means to avoid dying at the end of a rope. The Indians believed that when a man died, the soul escaped the body through the mouth. Death by strangulation, i.e. any death that cut off the windpipe, trapped the soul forever within the corpse and condemned it to a hellish existence.[1] Kicking Bird and Satanta hated each other. But for one brief moment on Grierson's front porch, Kicking Bird was ready to lay down his own life to save Satanta from the gallows.

Like Big Tree, Satanta recognized the inevitable domination of the whites. Unlike the younger chief, however, he refused to accept it. Wily and gifted, Satanta played both ends against the middle, mixing arrogance with humility, defiance with submission, always trying to keep his enemies off balance. In prison, he simply became indifferent. Finally, when he could no longer bend to the white will, he committed suicide and in this last show of defiance he was, once again, a true Kiowa warrior.

Whatever else he might have been, Satanta was one of the most complex men ever to rise from the plains, and there is a certain greatness about him.

Generations died and others took their place. The settlers of the West had dreaded the very names of the great war chiefs. Their descendants learned to respect them and even give them a grudging admiration. Geronimo's name became a battle cry of the same army that for so long had fought him. Jeff Chandler's portrayal of Cochise in the film *Broken Arrow* elevated the Chiricahua chief to a cult figure. It was time to end the old hatreds surrounding Satanta. In the spring of 1963, James Auchiah, his fifty-seven-year-old grandson, wrote Governor John Connally, asking for return of his bones to Oklahoma. Connally began working on the legislature which took up a resolution to repatriate his remains to the Kiowas.[2]

---

[1]Dodge, *Our Wild Indians*, 103.

[2]House Concurrent Resolution No. 67, Fifty-eighth Legislature, filed with the Secretary of State, May 20, 1863, copy in "Satanta" File, Center for American History.

The resolution did not pass without a fight. Memories are long in west Texas, and the representative from Parker County, so often the target of Kiowa raids, was vehement in his opposition. Still, it was approved by the House of Representatives on April 29, 1963, and by the Senate on May 2. On May 17, Connally signed it.[3]

In June, Auchiah appeared on Peckerwood Hill in Huntsville, dressed in the feather headdress and black and red robe of the Kiowa Gourd Dance Society. Around his neck was the peace medal Satanta had received at Medicine Lodge. He built a fire at the foot of the grave, then sprinkled it with cedar dust along with powdered granite from Mount Scott in Oklahoma, one of Satanta's favorite places.

"This ritual is called 'the smoking of the grave' and assures that the spirit of the departed will return to his homeland safely," he told a reporter from the Dallas *Times-Herald*. To the Dallas *Morning News'* Frank Tolbert, he added, "I could not go back to Oklahoma and report that I had failed to smoke my grandfather's grave. The smoking of a warrior's grave is one of the most ancient and most necessary of Kiowa ceremonies."

When the rites were finished, convicts opened the grave. There were a few bones, a square, hand-made nail and a few pieces of pottery. Gillett Griswold, director of the Fort Sill Museum, identified the bones as human. Joe Byrd, groundskeeper for the cemetery, said he was surprised there was anything left because the grave was shallow, and the soil, sandy and porous. The remains were placed in a plastic bag for shipment back to Oklahoma and burial with honors at Fort Sill.[4]

Satanta was going home at last.

---

[3]Ibid., Weems, *Death Song,* 267.
[4]Dallas *Morning News,* June 19, 1963; Dallas *Times-Herald,* June 30, 1963.

Bibliography

There is a large body of literature on the Indian Trial, but unfortunately it is scattered, mostly appearing as portions of books covering a much larger story.

The most significant work is W.S. Nye's *Carbine and Lance*. Although it is a history of Fort Sill from its founding into modern times, its coverage of the events leading to the Warren Wagon Train Massacre, the raid itself and the arrest of the chiefs is unparalleled and unlikely to be surpassed. Nye had the advantage of being stationed at Fort Sill some seventy years ago, when a few of the Indian participants were still alive, and so heard it first hand. Any gaps were filled by children of participants who got it from their fathers.

Ida Lasater Huckabay does well in *Ninety-four Years in Jack County*. As its title states, it is a purely local history from the Jack County point of view, has some inaccuracies, and does not attempt to go into Nye's exhaustive detail of events elsewhere. Still, it is essential reading for anyone interested in the raid and trial.

I am continually amazed that Benjamin Capps' *The Warren Wagontrain Raid* is still considered the definitive work on the subject. It is not history. It is a novel. Capps creates his own dialogue among the Indians for dramatic effect, just as Irving Stone and James A. Michener have created it for their various historical novels. In an apologia to a recent reprint of the book, Capps went so far as to call Lawrie Tatum a "dupe." This is certainly true of Enoch Hoag and James Haworth, but the record shows Tatum to have been entirely his own man and coldbloodedly realistic about his Indian charges. I did not rely on *The Warren Wagontrain Raid* for any portion of this work.

191

GOVERNMENT DOCUMENTS AND PUBLICATIONS

Day, James M. and Dorman Winfrey (senior eds). *Texas Indian Papers, 1860-1916.* Austin: Texas State Library, 1961.

Jack County. Minutes of the District Court. Vol. A. Office of the District Clerk. Jacksboro, Texas.

Mooney, James. *Calendar History of the Kiowa Indians.* 1898. Reprint. Washington: Smithsonian Institution Press, 1979.

___. "Kiowa." Frederick Webb Hodge, ed. *Handbook of American Indians North of Mexico.* Vol. 1. 1905. Reprint. Totowa, N.J: Rowman and Littlefield, 1975.

State of Texas. House Concurrent Resolution No. 67. Fifty-eighth Legislature. Filed with the Secretary of State, May 20, 1963.

Texas Prison Papers. Texas Prison Museum, Huntsville, Texas.

United States Department of the Interior. Bureau of Indian Affairs. Kiowa Agency, Federal, State and Local Court Relations, Trial of Satanta and Big Tree, May 30, 1871, to August 15, 1878. Indian Archives Division, Oklahoma Historical Society, Oklahoma City.

United States Department of War. Office of the Adjutant General. Record Group 94. Returns of U.S. Military Posts, Fort Richardson, Texas. Washington: National Archives Microfilm Publications. Vol. 617. Roll 1008.

___. Record Group 94 4447 Adjutant General's Office 1871. Letters Received. National Archives, Washington.

___. Record Group 391 Series 757. Fourth Cavalry Expedition Records. Letters Received and Endorsements Sent and Orders Issued, 1871-1872. National Archives, Washington.

___. Record Group 393. Special File. Military Division of the Missouri. Hancock's War. National Archives, Washington.

___. Post Medical Report, Fort Griffin, Texas. Microfilm copy in possession of Arnulfo Oliveira Library, University of Texas at Brownsville.

NON-GOVERNMENT MANUSCRIPT SOURCES AND SPECIAL FILES

Hamilton, Allen Lee. "Military History of Fort Richardson, Texas." MA Thesis, University of Texas at Arlington, July 1973.

Mackenzie, Ranald Slidell. Letterbook. Thomas Gilcrease Institute. Tulsa, Oklahoma.

Myers, James Will. Papers. Panhandle-Plains Historical Society. Canyon, Texas.

Nohl, Lessing H., Jr. "Bad Hand: The Military Career of Ranald Slidell

Mackenzie, 1871-1889." PhD. dissertation, University of New Mexico, 1962.

Pate, J'Nell Laverne. "Colonel Ranald Slidell Mackenzie's First Four Years in the Fourth Cavalry in Texas, 1871-1874." MA Thesis, Texas Christian University, August 1963.

Rister, Carl C. Papers. Southwestern Collection. Texas Tech University, Lubbock, Texas.

"Satanta." Vertical file. Center for American History. University of Texas, Austin.

Sherman, William Tecumseh. Unofficial Correspondence. Library of Congress, Washington.

NEWSPAPERS

Army and Navy Journal.

Austin *State Journal.*

Cincinnati *Commercial.*

Dallas *Morning News.*

Dallas *Time-Herald.*

New York *Times.*

St. Louis *Missouri Democrat.*

San Antonio *Express.*

BOOKS—PRIMARY

Battey, Thomas C. *The Life and Adventures of a Quaker Among the Indians.* 1875. Reprint. Williamstown, Mass.: Corner House Publishers, 1972.

Carter, Robert G. *The Old Sergeant's Story: Fighting Indians and Bad Men in Texas From 1870 to 1876.* 1926 Reprint. Mattituck, N.Y. and Bryan, Texas: J.M. Carroll and Company, 1982.

___. *On the Border with Mackenzie, or Winning the West from the Comanches.* 1935. Reprint. New York: Antiquarian Press, 1961.

Dixon, Olive K. *Life of "Billy" Dixon.* 1927. Reprint. Austin: State House Press, 1987.

Dodge, Richard Irving. *Our Wild Indians: Thirty-Three Years' Personal Experience Among the Red Men of the Great West.* Hartford, Conn.: A.D. Worthington and Co., 1882.

Grant, U.S. *Personal Memoirs.* 2 vols. New York: Charles L. Webster and Company, 1886.

Kellogg, M.K. *M.K. Kellogg's Texas Journal.* ed. by Llerena Friend. Austin: University of Texas Press, 1972.

Lowe, Percival G. *Five Years a Dragoon ('49 to '54) and Other Adventures on the Great Plains.* Kansas City: The Franklin Hudson Publishing Co., 1906.

McConnell, H.H. *Five Years a Cavalryman*. Jacksboro, Texas: J.N. Rogers and Co., 1889.

Pratt, Richard Henry. *Battlefield and Classroom*. ed. by Robert Utley. New Haven: Yale University Press, 1964.

Sherman, William Tecumseh. *Memoirs of General W.T. Sherman*. Rev. ed. 1886. Reprint. New York: Library of America, 1990.

Stanley, Henry M. *My Early Travels and Adventures in America*. 1895. Reprint. Lincoln: University of Nebraska Press, 1982.

Strong, Henry W. *My Frontier Days & Indian Fights on the Plains of Texas*. Dallas: Privately printed, 1926.

Tatum, Lawrie. *Our Red Brothers and the Peace Policy of President Ulysses S. Grant*. 1899. Reprint. Lincoln: University of Nebraska Press, 1970.

BOOKS—SECONDARY

Berthrong, Donald J. *The Southern Cheyennes*. Norman: University of Oklahoma Press, 1963.

Haley, James L. *The Buffalo War: The History of the Red River Indian Uprising of 1874*. 1976. Reprint. Norman: University of Oklahoma Press, 1985.

Hamilton, Allen Lee. *Sentinel of the Southern Plains: Fort Richardson and the Northwest Texas Frontier, 1866-1878*. Fort Worth: Texas Christian University Press, 1988.

Hoig, Stan. *The Battle of the Washita: The Sheridan Custer Indian Campaign of 1867–69*. Garden City: Doubleday and Company, 1976.

Huckabay, Ida Lasater. *Ninety-four Years in Jack County*. Austin: Steck Company, 1948.

Hutton, Paul Andrew. *Phil Sheridan and His Army*. Lincoln: University of Nebraska Press, 1985.

Jones, Douglas C. *The Treaty of Medicine Lodge: The Story of the Great Treaty Council as Told by Eyewitnesses*. Norman: University of Oklahoma Press, 1966.

Ledbetter, Barbara A. Neal. *Fort Belknap, Frontier Saga: Indians, Negroes and Anglo-Americans on the Texas Frontier*. Burnet, Texas: Eakin Press, 1982.

Mayhall, Mildred. *The Kiowas*. Norman: University of Oklahoma Press, 1971.

Newcomb, W.W., Jr. *The Indians of Texas*. Austin: University of Texas Press, 1961.

BIBLIOGRAPHY

Nye, Wilbur S. Carbine and Lance: *The Story of Old Fort Sill.* 1937. Reprint. Norman: University of Oklahoma Press, 1969.

Prucha, Francis Paul. *The Great Father: The United States Government and the American Indians.* Abridge edition. Lincoln: University of Nebraska Press, 1986.

Ramsdell, Charles William. *Reconstruction in Texas.* Austin: University of Texas Press, 1970.

Robinson, Charles M., III. *Bad Hand: A Biography of General Ranald S. Mackenzie.* Austin: State House Press, 1993.

___. *The Buffalo Hunters.* Austin: State House Press, 1995.

Weems, John Edward. *Death Song: The Last of the Indian Wars.* New York: Indian Head Books, 1991.

Wellman, Paul I. *Death in the Desert: The Fifty Years' War for the Great Southwest.* 1935 Reprint. Lincoln: University of Nebraska Press, 1987.

Wharton, Clarence. *Satanta, the Great Chief of the Kiowas and His People.* Dallas: Banks Upshaw and Company, 1935.

Wilbarger, J.W. *Indian Depredations in Texas.* 1889. Reprint. Austin: Eakin Press and State House Books, 1985.

ARTICLES

Butler, Josiah. "Pioneer School Teaching at the Comanche-Kiowa Agency School 1870-3." *Chronicles of Oklahoma.* Vol. 6, No. 4. (1928)

Carter, Robert G. "The Cowboys' Verdict." H.H. McConnell. *Five Years a Cavalryman.* Jacksboro, Texas: J.N. Rogers and Co., 1889.

Coonfield, Ed. "The Fine Art of Hanging." *Real West.* Vol. 29, No. 211 (December 1986).

Doan, C.F. "Reminiscences of the Old Trails." J. Marvin Hunter (comp.). *The Trail Drivers of Texas.* 1924. Reprint. Austin: University of Texas, 1985.

Morris, W.A. "Big Tree's Raid in Montague County." *Frontier Times.* Vol. 5, No. 1 (October 1927).

Richardson, Rupert N. "The Comanche Indians and the Fight at Adobe Walls." *Panhandle-Plains Historical Review.* Vol. 4 (1931).

Rister, C.C., ed. "Documents Relating to General W.T. Sherman[']s Southern Plains Indian Policy 1871-1875." *Panhandle-Plains Historical Review.* Vol. 9 (1936) and Vol. 10 (1937).

Robinson, Charles M., III. "Kicking Bird, Kiowa Martyr for Peace." *True West.* Vol. 4, No. 1 (January 1993).

___. "The Tough Little Ranger of Lost Valley." *True West* Vol. 38, No. 8 (August 1991).

Wallace, Ernest, ed. "Ranald S. Mackenzie's Official Correspondence Relating to Texas, 1871-1873." *The Museum Journal.* Vol. 9 (1965).

___. "Ranald S. Mackenzie's Official Correspondence Relating to Texas, 1873-1879. *The Museum Journal.* Vol. 10 (1966).

Index

Adobe Walls, Tex: 169

A'do-eete: *see Big Tree*

Agencies, Indian: Cheyenne Agency, 169n, 176; Kiowa-Comanche Agency (Fort Sill Agency), 12, 39-42, 46-49, 69, 70, 76, 119, 128, 137, 144, 161, 173, 182; Wichita Agency, 55, 72, 130, 170, 176

Alabama and Coushatta Indians: 126

Alvord, H. E: 132; advice to Davis, 147-48

Anadarko, Okla.: 141, 170, 182

Antelope Hills: 77

Apache Indians: 185, *see also Kiowa-Apache Indians.*

Arapaho Indians: 30, 55, 116, 168, 170, 174, 175

Arkansas River: 20

Army and Navy Journal: 84

Atkins, J. D. C: 186

Atkinson, Jehu: 97

Atoka, Okla: 131-32

A'to-t'ain: 171, 171n

Auchiah, James: 188-89

Augur, Christopher C: 128, 149n, 174-75

Austin, Tex., *State Journal:* 45, 97, 111, 111n

Bailey, Dave: 173

Ball, Thomas: 104, 108n, 109, 111; opening statement at trial, 104-05n

Baxter, N. J: 71, 99, 127

Battey, Thomas: 136, 144, 160n, 169; becomes hostage, 138-39n, 143

Beals, Private: 92

Beede, Cyrus: 130, 132, 137, 143

Belknap, William W: 114, 123

Big Bear: 120

Big Bow: 77-78, 111, 127, 146

Big Jake: 118

Big Tree (A'do-eete): 15, 56, 90, 115ff, 131-33, 162-63, 183, 187-88; and Warren Massacre, 56n, 65-66, 77-78; arrest of, 80-81; transported to Texas, 91ff; age of, 92-92n; indicted for murder, 99-100; trial of, 103ff, 108n, security arrangements for, 103; convicted and sentenced, 109, 111; sentence commuted, 112-113; sent to penitentiary, 113-14, 124n; in prison, 124 ff; freedom for, 130, 135 ff; transported to Fort Sill, 146; and Fort Sill council, 149ff; paroled, 160-61; and Red River War, 175ff; converts to Christianity, 184-85; death of, 185

Big Wichita River: 71, 72

Black Eagle: *see Eagle Heart*

Black Fox (novel and television mini-series): 25n

Black Hills, South Dakota: 20

Black Kettle: 26, 86

Boehm, Peter Martin: 72

Bowlegs, Billy: 26-27

Bowman, James: 71, 99, 127

Braun, Matt: 25n

Brazeal, Thomas: 68, 79, 105

Brazos River: 72, 174

Broken Arrow (film): 188

Brown, Daniel: 104

Brown, George: 36n

Brown, John H: 104

Bryant, Joe: 181-82

Buchanan, James: 30

Buell, George: 174

Buffalo Creek: 121

Buffalo Goad: 155

INDEX

Mackenzie, Ranald Slidell: 61-62, 75, 84, 89-90, 105, 107, 109, 113, 129, 157; background, 51-52, pursues raiders, 68ff; returns chiefs to Texas, 90ff; views on Indian suppression, 122; 1871 Indian campaigns, 123-24, 127-28; Sherman's opinion of, 124n; attack on Comanche camp, 135; and Red River War, 174-75; death of, 183

McConnell, W. M: 58, 63, 111n

McCusker, Philip: 148, 160-61

Mamaday-te (Young Lone Wolf): 173

Maman-ti (Do-ha-te, Sky-Walker): 60, 72, 122, 171ff; character, 56; as war leader, 56-57, 117; and Warren Massacre, 58ff; and Davidson, 117-18; transported to Florida, 179-80; death of, 181

Marcy, Randolph B: 52, 59, 62; notes Indian devastation, 61; and arrest of chiefs, 79

Medicine Lodge Treaty: *see Treaties*

Menard, Tex: 25, 56

Mexican War: 24

Miles, John D: 150, 170

Miles, Nelson A: 174-75

Military Division of the Missouri: 86

Missouri River: 19, 130

Modoc Indians: 137ff

Montague County, Tex: 45, 123, 185

Morris, W. A: 181-82

Mooney, James: 21-22

Mullen (Mullins), John: 71, 99, 127

Myers, James Will: 54, 83; on Kiowa customs, 22; on Indian grievances, 23n

Nap-a-wat: 171

Neill, Thomas: 176

New York *Times:* 112

Nez Perce Indians: 176, 185

Nicholson, William: 103, 133

Ninth United States Cavalry: 128

Nye, Wilbur Sturtevant: 96n, 173n; researches Warren Massacre, 56n, 81n

O'Daniel, W. Lee: 183n

Oklahoma (Indian Territory): agencies in, 38ff; and throughout

Okmulgee, Okla: 55, 139

Ord-lee: 66, 68, 172

Osage Indians: 23, 30

Otter Creek, Okla: 89

Oxford, Trumpter: 95

Pacer: 119-20, 154

Palo Duro Canyon, Tex: battle of, 175

Palo Pinto County, Tex: 41

Parker County, Tex: 41, 45, 69, 99

Parker, Ely S: 101-102n

Parker, Quanah: 127, 168, 179

Parra-o-coom: 111

Patzki, Julius H: 70

Penn, William: 38

Philadelphia, Penn: 98, 164

Platte River: 19

Pocahontas: 105

P'oinkia: 184

Pope, John: 76, 149n

Porter, Mel: 173

Pratt, Richard: 80

Price, William R: 174-75

Quahadi Comanches: *see* Comanche Indians—Quahadi band

Quakers: *see Society of Friends*

Quirts Quip: 154-55

Quitan: 72

Rainy Mountain Creek, Okla: 89

Red River: 23, 40, 56-57, 72, 89-90, 110, 115, 121, 135, 144, 170, 174-75, 181

Red River War: 166n, 174ff, 179, 183

Reynolds, Joseph J: 112, 113, 123, 126-28

Rio Grande: 19, 85, 130, 136

Richards, Jonathan: 81n, 130, 141, 150, 170

Rister, Carl Coke: 108n

Roessler, Professor: 43

Robinson, Corporal: 92, 94

Robinson, J. R: 63

Ross, Edmund: 31-32

St. Louis, Mo: 132, 147

St. Louis *Missouri Democrat:* 29, 36n

Salt Creek Prairie, Tex: 52, 58, 60-61, 68, 172

San Antonio, Tex: 56, 114, 128

CPSIA information can be obtained
at www.ICGtesting.com
Printed in the USA
FFOW04n0149290316
22758FF